UNBELIEVING HUSBANDS
AND THE WIVES WHO LOVE THEM

Unbelieving Husbands and the Wives Who Love Them

MICHAEL J. FANSTONE

Servant Publications
Ann Arbor, Michigan

Vine Books is an imprint of Servant Publications especially
designed to serve evangelical Christians.

Unless otherwise noted, all Scripture references were taken from
the New International Version of the Bible. All rights reserved.

This book was originally released in 1994 by Monarch
Publications (England) under the title *Together Apart*.

Although the men and women whose stories are told in this book
are real, all names have been changed to protect the privacy of
those involved.

Published by Servant Publications
P.O. Box 8617
Ann Arbor, Michigan 48107

Cover design: Diane Bareis
Cover illustrations: Hile Illustration & Design, Ann Arbor, Michigan

96 97 98 99 00 10 9 8 7 6 5 4 3

Printed in the United States of America
ISBN 0-89283-940-6

Library of Congress Cataloging-In-Publication Data

Fanstone, Michael J. (Micahel John)
    Unbelieving husbands and the wives who love them / Michael J.
Fanstone.
       p. cm.
    Rev. ed. of : Together apart. 1994
    Includes bibliographical references and index.
    ISBN 0-89283-940-6
    1. Wives—Religious life. 2. Husbands—Religious life. 3.
Witness bearing (Christianity) 4. Marriage—Religious aspects—
Christianity. I. Fanstone, Michael J. (Michael John), 1948—Together
apart. II. Title.
BV4527.F364 1996
248.4—dc20   95-44472
                                                              CIP

Contents

Acknowledgements

I accept full responsibility for the contents of this book. If you find it unhelpful or insensitive, therefore, the blame falls solidly on my shoulders.

This has not been a solo project on my part, however, and there are a number of people whose contributions have been invaluable.

Research. A number of ministers and church leaders responded positively to my appeal for help and asked some Christian wives in their congregations if they would complete one of my questionnaires. I appreciate this, as I do the cooperation of the editors of two British Christian publications: Elizabeth Round (*Woman Alive*); and Bruce Hardy (*Christian Herald*). Both printed my invitation for Christian wives with uncommitted husbands to contact me if they were prepared to cooperate.

Contributors. As a result of these initiatives, many women sent me completed questionnaires, and some of them managed as well to get their husbands and children to fill in different versions. This material, from so many cooperative people, has helped me to understand much better the circumstances of women and their families in this situation.

Improvements to the text. A number of people have helped graciously in various ways ever since I produced the first draft of the material. I am grateful to Rosemary Green, Emmanuel

Baptist Church's office secretary, who has provided valuable help with my research work. I am also indebted to others as well: Marion Sherwood, Valeria Brigden, Dr. Lindsay Kemp, Jenny Miller, Irene Archer, Sylvia Austen, Graham Flatman, and Lilian and Derek Cook of Maranatha Ministries. Each one has made helpful and constructive suggestions about the content and style of the text. However, Marion and David Thompson deserve a special mention for the meticulous way in which they proofread the whole manuscript and advocated numerous improvements.

To each of the above, and to God, who I believe gave me the vision, motivation, time, and stamina to undertake this project, I want to communicate my sincere thanks. I know that readers who appreciate any of this material will join me in expressing gratitude too.

Michael J. Fanstone

Introduction

In the average church there are more women than men. Half of these women probably come to church without a male companion. Some are single, but others have a husband at home who does not share their Christian faith. Their faith is important to them, but at home they may have to keep it to themselves. Possibly you are one of them.

Now in her sixties, Jean became a Christian when she had been married for twenty-five years. She was exasperated with a drunken husband who treated home like a hotel, and she frequently had tension headaches through trying to cope with two unhappy teenagers. Her husband did not allow her new-found faith to interfere with him in any way and always scoffed at her when he noticed the changes in her life. Eighteen years later, Jean says, "His attitude toward me has not changed for the better." She knows her painful experience will continue.

Husbands respond in a variety of ways to their wives' faith. Some do not object to their wives going to church and having Christian friends, and may be perfectly happy to attend church at certain times of the year themselves. Others may be comparatively content for their wives to go to church on a Sunday, but are none too pleased if home and family life are affected. The most extreme reaction is found in husbands who either cannot or will not understand even a little about the Christian faith and church. If they also have a tendency to get jealous, they may object violently to their wives having a relationship with another man—even if his name is Jesus and he lives a safe distance away in heaven! They may also be unhappy about their wives having other close relationships outside the family.

In many marriages one partner believes and trusts in Jesus Christ and the other does not. *If this is your situation, you are not alone.* Usually the wife is the believer, but there are also homes where the husband has found Christ, but his wife has not. While I have written this book principally for women in this situation, there is also plenty of material that applies to men in these circumstances.

You may wonder why a man would write a book for women. After all, I have never been married to an unbelieving husband! As the minister of a local church, however, I have met many wives whose husbands do not yet believe in Jesus. They tell me that if they try to talk to their partner about anything religious, it is often as if they are speaking different languages. This is no one's fault; it is simply the way it is. I come to this subject, therefore, with some awareness of the pain and frustration of wives. I have been helped enormously during my research and writing, however, by the way they have shared their own experiences and situations with me.

My research involved questionnaires that were distributed widely throughout the United Kingdom and Ireland. Throughout the book I have been able to relate real stories from people who live, or have lived, under pressure because of a spiritual division in their relationships and homes. I am very grateful to those who have helped me. Although these women have granted me permission to use their stories, I have changed some names to protect the contributor's anonymity.

My wife's comments and responses have helped me greatly. Diane read each section as I finished it. She has been involved, probably more than I have, in ministry to and with wives whose partners do not yet believe in Jesus. In many respects, therefore, we have undertaken a joint project, and I am deeply grateful for her help.

I have attempted to explore the situation from all sides and have discovered much pain and heartache. Christian women have felt isolated, ostracized, and judged at church because they come without a partner. Surrounded by apparently happy couples, they often feel condemned and excluded. Yet, deep inside, they feel helpless to change their situation. Most would be thrilled if their husbands would come to church, but for the time being this seems out of the question, and the anguish goes on.

God has always known how much pain married couples would suffer if they were divided about something very important. When he created human beings and instituted marriage, both Adam and Eve had an identical faith and trust in him. They shared not only a relationship together but also a relationship with God. He knew that if only one of them trusted him, it would lead to division within their marriage. This is why the Bible strongly discourages marriages between a person with a living faith in God and one without (Ezra 9:1-4; 2 Cor 6:14-18).

God intends marriage to draw a man and woman together in a formal relationship of mutual love and commitment. This relationship should satisfy the needs of both partners and create an ideal environment into which children may be born and nurtured. God's desire is that there should be united, loving, and stable family units, in which people are genuinely happy, into which he is welcomed, and in which he is loved and honored.

God's ideal is often thwarted, however. Some couples are divided because a Christian fell in love with someone with whom he or she had nothing in common spiritually. Alternatively, it may be that both husband and wife were equally committed to Christ when they married, but one of them has since fallen away. Often it is because, after marrying as unbelievers, the husband or wife was introduced to Jesus Christ and became committed to him. Ironically, while this brings that person alive spiritually, it can introduce painful tensions into the marriage. All too soon it becomes apparent why the Bible, while obviously encouraging people to turn to Christ, makes it clear that what we call "unequal yoking" is not ideal.

It is not just wives who suffer. I have come across husbands who thought their marriages were happy and stable, yet were plunged into chaos when their wives began to follow Jesus Christ. Others found their wives' conversion made a less obvious difference, and indeed provoked them to reflect carefully on what, if anything, they believed. What affects many husbands most is not their wives' newfound faith, but the wives' insistence on giving the local church some of their time, energy, and money. This often appears provocative and divisive.

In this book I will attempt to be at the same time realistic, practical, and spiritual. You will find no triumphalistic theology which assumes that all you have to do is pray and witness, and an unbelieving husband will fall on his knees in submission to Jesus. I will discuss how we can work in partnership with God so that unconverted husbands or wives have the opportunity to get to know him personally. I will not assume, however, that there is a method or technique we can use which guarantees that an unbeliever will come to faith. No such method exists. I will also explore how to manage the problems of bringing up children when husband and wife have different perspectives on spiritual matters. Finally, I will examine how the local church can help wives with unbelieving husbands.

God works in a multitude of ways that do not always make sense to us. When one partner finds Christ, it sometimes contributes toward the end of that marriage. This is not easy to cope with or accept, yet in the real world it happens. God often uses hard times and trauma to encourage us to trust him because no one and nothing else can sustain us. In practice this means that a Christian wife may find her spiritual life deepens more if her husband does not come to faith immediately than if he does!

We would like to see marriages unified as unbelieving partners start to trust Jesus for themselves, but some wives will never experience this joyful event. If they count on this happening, they may become increasingly disillusioned and disheartened. I will therefore discuss how they can find God's peace in less than ideal circumstances.

I hope that this book will be used by God to minister pastorally to a part of his church that is often in pain. I do not pretend to have all the answers. Some of the real-life situations that I describe do not appear to have any simple solution. I wish they did, but our calling is to cope with difficulties as God supports and encourages us.

I pray that God will speak to you, reassure you, and encourage you as you read this book. Should it help you in any way or if you have personal insights and experiences to share, I would be grateful and glad to hear from you, in writing, via the publisher.

Michael J. Fanstone
Gravesend, England 1994

PART ONE

All About You

CHAPTER ONE

What Are You Going Through?

I suspect you wish that you did not have to read this book. You feel that if your husband would believe in Jesus as you do, many of your current problems would be solved. You find it hard to be a Christian at home—it is probably the toughest place to live out your faith. Maybe you and your husband find it virtually impossible to communicate over anything spiritual—just like two people who cannot grasp each other's language. Indeed, for you it may even be worse! Your Christian faith and your trust and belief in God is important to you and has made a noticeable difference in your life, but it is not something the two of you can share. You know that your faith has introduced, or aggravated, a problem in your relationship. This makes things rather delicate.

The Bible teaches us a lot about marriage, especially that it was a part of God's plan for the human race. Having created mankind (Gn 1:27), God established a pattern for the most important human relationship on earth. "A man will leave his father and mother and be united to his wife, and they will become one flesh" (Gn 2:24). The relationship of dependency on parents is superseded by a relationship of love, trust, and sexual union with husband or wife. It is in this environment that children are to be born and raised (Gn 1:28).

Probably the most important words in Genesis 2:24 are those that describe marriage as "united" and "one flesh." Marriage is about two people coming together in a deep and intimate way to share life. The implication is that they should love each other deeply, trust one another, be committed to each other for the rest of their lives, be open and honest with one another in everything, and, as a practical expression of all this, show their love for each other in sexual union. When marriage is truly like this, it is joyful, deeply pleasurable, and fulfilling.

COMMON PROBLEMS

So many things can go wrong and often do. As we identify some of the most common problems, we need to recognize that any combination of these may be found in some situations.

Lack of Communication. Some marriages collapse when the husband and wife stop communicating, and relate only at a superficial level. Some couples have never related deeply, even during their courtship. Dr. Lawrence Crabb tells of a couple who came to him for marriage counseling. The wife told him, "We get along—but from a distance. I can never tell him how I really feel about anything. He always gets mad and jumps at me, or he clams up for a couple of days. I don't think we've ever had a really close communication."[1]

If a husband or wife suppresses hurt, pain, or anger toward the other person because open expression is too difficult, it is hardly surprising if the marriage slips steadily downhill until a crisis occurs. By then, great damage may have been done.

Lack of trust. Most couples trust each other when they marry. We expect our partner to be faithful to us indefinitely. This commitment is essential. A flight attendant explains, "After six years of living with a man, I decided that I wanted to be married. Since the fellow I was living with liked our no-strings-attached arrangement, I found somebody else who was willing to tie the knot, and we got married two months ago. So far it's great!"[2]

Despite the vows made at weddings, many people who commit themselves to one partner ultimately betray him or her. Many people who thought they could trust their partner have been deeply hurt. Sexual infidelity and financial irresponsibility, for example, are areas of life where one partner's lack of self-discipline can lead to the other partner experiencing great pain. Trust has been destroyed, and many in this situation feel it is impossible for it to be rebuilt.

Growing apart. Other couples just drift away from each other as time goes on. It is not that they do not love each other anymore, or have endless arguments. Rather, they begin to live separate lives. If one puts career advancement, for example, as a priority, it tends to have this effect. Sometimes a hobby or leisure activity becomes all-important. Anything that divides a couple, intentionally or not, may have a serious and negative effect on the relationship.

One of the most enjoyable aspects of my work as a minister is premarital counseling. I insist on at least three two-hour sessions with every couple whom I will later join in marriage. One future bridegroom, Steve, told me recently, "My friends don't understand me when I tell them that I'm going to marry my best friend!" Yet this is the kind of relationship that should be at the heart of every marriage. When both partners have gone their own ways and have little in common, the relationship is in jeopardy.

Kathleen explains what caused this in her marriage. "My becoming a Christian has meant leading separate lives, with different values and differing sources of enjoyment."[3]

Irene's experience is similar. Her husband told her, "Our interests are so different, this marriage is a waste of time."

Domestic tensions. Many marriages collapse when pressures at home become unbearable. Financial difficulties are a major source of stress, and layoffs, unemployment, or early retirement can force a couple to spend far more time locked in each other's company than is wise or healthy. Without the fulfillment and satisfaction of work a person can be hard to live with, and if the money coming into the home is severely limited, it can easily lead to irritability, anger, and resentment from either partner. In such circumstances, one of them may feel forced to leave.

Spiritual separation. Any marriage can be strained if there are major differences between the two partners. I know a number of couples where the husbands and wives are from different parts of the world. This means that their first languages and background cultures are very different. The only way their marriages can be strong and secure is if they work hard at listening, being patient, and trying to understand their partners. At least, though, they came into the marriage knowing that these differences existed.

The same is not the case when two unbelievers marry and one starts to attend Christian meetings that do not appeal in the least to the other. This has the effect of creating, almost overnight, a gulf between the two of them. If one partner then makes a commitment of his or her life to God, the gulf widens. They now have different priorities in life and think in different ways. The way they choose to spend their time and money may be at variance.

DEEP FEELINGS

It may help at this stage if we identify some of the feelings experienced by Christian wives in this situation, for two main reasons. First, we need to show what is predictable in such circumstances. You will be encouraged to see that you are responding perfectly naturally and normally when you find the way you feel listed here. Many other wives have felt the same way. Second, it is important to identify and clarify your feelings. When life is demanding, it is not always easy to separate the mixed reactions you experience.

Inadequacy. It is not at all unusual for a Christian wife to believe firmly that she is to blame if her husband has not yet come to faith. If only she witnessed better at home, if only she stopped losing her temper so easily, if only she had more courage to tell him about Jesus, if she were a better Christian, he would have believed by now. Melanie says, "I find it difficult when I see what a marvelous Christian he would make if he accepted the Lord, but there are many times when I feel I fail by not giving him a good example." Another wife feels that people blame her for the fact that her husband is not a Christian.

This sense of blame, inadequacy, and condemnation is regrettable and unnecessary in the opinion of Derek and Lilian Cook, who present seminars on this subject. They begin their teaching with the following (very firm) message, "If you are a wife who is a Christian and your husband is not, it is *not* all your fault."[4]

Loneliness. The single people in many churches often tend to be either young and unattached or older and bereaved. In this environment, single, middle-aged adults can feel isolated and excluded. This includes those who have never been married, those who are separated, divorced, or widowed, and those who are married but not joined at church by their partner. Such single adults feel left out despite the fact that there are many people around. Many activities seem geared for couples, families, young people, or older people. Socializing with couples is hard because they tend to prefer to spend time with other couples. Christian wives whose husbands do not share their faith do not just feel lonely at church. Jasmine says, "I have a feeling of loneliness at home with God being such a large part of my life, yet I can't share him in words with my husband." Maxine agrees. "I feel lonely and isolated because my husband has no concept of a spiritual life." Sophie finds that she needs her Christian friends. "Sometimes I feel very lonely, but God is kind and has provided the help I need via other wives in the same situation." Christine's perspective is slightly different. "I feel very lonely spiritually and my Christian friendships become too important to me, which makes my husband feel left out." Those who feel lonely sometimes have very difficult decisions to make.

Torn loyalties. Differences of opinion about any number of issues is highly likely when one partner in a marriage has become a Christian and the other has not. For Dave, the Christian in his home, the difficulties are over how his family spends Sundays. He says:

I always feel I'm running on half-power as a Christian, because I can't bring my faith into my family life. I usually go to church on Sunday mornings, where I'm in the music group, and occasionally to house group [small group] meetings. But sometimes I stay at home on Sunday mornings so we can be a family together.[5]

Alison's problem is more general: "I am being dragged in two different directions all the time, and virtually have to put my faith to one side to avoid any conflicts." Avril finds it difficult in specific ways. "Our opinions and the way we use our time is different. He wants to watch TV and go to the bar but I want to serve God with my time and not always be watching TV. I find it especially hard to go to the bar. Also, there is a whole part of me that I can't share with him and I would like to serve the Lord in more ways, but I have to respect my husband's wishes."

Fear. Christians with an uncommitted partner sometimes experience fear. It can be provoked, as in Margaret's case, by the prospect of disagreements at home. "I don't flaunt my beliefs," she says. "It means on many occasions I have to compromise by not going to meetings at church because I fear the argument at home if I say I'm going."

Other wives have a very real fear about eternity. Jesus tells us that he is preparing "a place" for us in heaven if we are his disciples (Jn 14:2). Revelation, the last New Testament book, gives us insight into God's heavenly kingdom. It is a place of worship, characterized by joy, and God intends those who believe in Jesus to look forward to going there. If, however, our marriage partners do not accept the Christian faith, we have to face the fact that the Bible says that they will not be there (Jn 3:16-18). This quite naturally provokes anxiety, fear, and considerable pain.

Christine's fear is intense. "I hate to think that if he is not saved he will go to hell," she says. Wendy's feelings are much the same. The fact that her husband is not a Christian makes her "so very sad—the alternative is everlasting death and this is hard to cope with." Another wife tells how she worries that if her husband dies in an accident she is unsure of where he will go.

Guilt. Christian wives whose husbands do not share their faith find many things make them feel guilty before God. Fiona feels guilty when she goes to church in the evenings. Wendy speaks of "my guilt when I am doing something for the Lord when I should perhaps be at home—all self-induced! My husband really doesn't mind, but I still feel guilty." Alison's situation is the opposite. "I feel guilty because I can't get involved in many of the activities arranged for church members," she says. Rosemary feels sad, and "guilty because I feel I should have done more to convince my husband about becoming a Christian."

A Christian wife alone in church often feels uncomfortable when the collection plate is passed. Unless she has her own income, she is unable to give much, if anything at all, and so she may feel uneasy and guilty. Following a survey of some of its readers with husbands who do not believe, *Christian Family* reported that some wives face "active opposition" over finances. The writer explained, "Understandably, many husbands are not prepared to see a tenth of their earnings go to the church."[6] However, this does not lessen the feelings of guilt in the Christian wife who strongly suspects that others in the church are giving far more sacrificially in response to God's love than she is able to do.

Frustration. Frustration is common among Christians whose partners do not share their faith. When we have known God personally for a while and our faith makes sense to us and helps us in our daily lives, we can find it hard to grasp why someone else who has been exposed to it cannot accept it and trust God as we do.

Wendy has often wondered about this. "My husband, who is not yet a Christian, attends church on Sunday mornings regularly and has done so for about seven years now, which is very frustrating." When asked how she feels about the fact that her husband is not yet a Christian, Sophie speaks of her frustration that the two of them cannot share the same thing. Susanna says, "The closer to the Lord my husband gets, the more frustrated I become. I have to keep reminding myself that it's not my problem and that he will get there in the Lord's time, not mine." Ruth's frustration is that her husband "cannot see how lovely Jesus is." Joanne's frustration is more practical: "being allowed to attend church only every other Sunday morning and not being able to attend Christian functions."

Resentment. Perpetual frustration can have a deeper effect in people's lives. They get to a point where things become tiresome and they begin to feel resentful. Jenny gets resentful sometimes when she cannot attend some meetings. She copes with these feelings through prayer and by trying to be aware of her husband's needs as well as her own.

The problems Beth has to cope with at home make her feel resentful, too:

> My husband is jealous of my being a Christian, of my friends who are Christians, and of the different person I have become because I am a Christian. He has different standards and told me off for indoctrinating the children when I had quiet times with them. He does not want to change his lifestyle. His bar, his friends, and his culture are too important to him. I feel resentment and anger which then turns to guilt. My husband likes to make me feel guilty. I then try to throw all these feelings back to God, and to lean on him so that I can forgive my husband.

Josie's resentment is directed more specifically. She says, "Sometimes I feel very angry with God! I have to trust his timing but I think it weakens my purpose in his work because of the dichotomy. There must be some purpose for this circumstance, but I'll be darned if I can see it. I tend to try to carry on regardless but am aware we're missing something."

The resentment Kathleen has to cope with is not her own but her husband's. She says:

> I used to resent John's refusal to come to God which, I felt, stood in my way of my finding a place in the church.... As the years go by, I've accepted that I am only able to join in the fellowship on the occasional Sunday morning. Sometimes I want to go, but get weary at the unspoken resentment and just can't face the sulky atmosphere if I do.[7]

Alienation. A Christian married to an unbeliever often feels separated from other people, both at church and at home. At church, a Christian wife feels she is at a disadvantage when trying to develop relationships. Sue says, "I started going to a small group to try to bridge the gap because I do feel very cut off at times."

Fiona, whose husband was a practicing Christian until the past few years, explains the difference this has made to her relationships at church:

> It's difficult coping with the loss of friendships. We were so heavily involved when we were Sunday school teachers and took the children on outings with other leaders. We organized social evenings and coffee after church, but now we have given it all up. We don't go to the social events much and I suppose it was only by going to these that we shared in the fellowship with others. I don't really like going to events on my own so we seem to have stopped socializing to a certain extent. I only stay for coffee after church if my son and daughter-in-law are with me.

At home, these wives find that things are different in their relationship with their partner because they *themselves* have changed. This can cause real strain. Kathleen adds,

> One issue I've had to face over the years is whether to join him in social events. I don't enjoy all the drinking and smutty jokes, and I feel that in the eyes of his friends I'm a wet blanket, which makes it difficult for John.[8]

Sexual tension. When a person becomes a Christian, that person starts being able to hear God and understand his mind. God reveals his intentions for our lives in the Bible, and one thing we discover there is that our sexuality was part of his plan for us. The Bible contains evidence of this in Song of Songs 2:3-17; 4:1-7, and Proverbs 5:18-19.

However, God intends sexual intercourse to be restricted to husband and wife as an expression of the love that bonds them in marriage. Within these parameters they have plenty of freedom, so long as both partners feel comfortable with what they do.

After a husband or a wife becomes a Christian, certain former sexual practices may begin to feel unsuitable. Should the Christian now feel convicted to stop participating in some of these, it may provoke protests from his or her partner.

Sadness. According to *Christian Family*, the most common difficulty facing Christian wives with husbands who do not share their faith is the inability to share fully with the most important person in her life.[9] This means that because the couple "looks at things from different standpoints" they are "unable to make prayerful decisions together." This is sad and yet, under the circumstances, inevitable. It is a source of great pain for the Christian partner who knows how different things could be.

Many wives have expressed this. Rachel says, "The fact my husband is not a Christian breaks my heart. If anything happened to him I would have no certainty of ever meeting him again. As a believer, I believe all who have rejected Jesus Christ will be in a lost eternity." Irene's husband is not a Christian and consequently she is very sad. "It would make such a wonderful difference to our relationship and draw us closer together in a way we have never known before." Maxine says she is "terribly sad because he is so obviously in bondage and relies on his own strength of character to solve problems. He seems very dark to me and I cry out to God to save him." Another wife tells how she is "sad, very sad. I know that he would feel he is a better person and be more confident in himself. He would also have a father whom he has never known because when he was a baby his father left his mother."

Christian wives whose husbands do not share their faith can

be pain-filled people. Linda Davis is probably correct when she says that "no segment of the church is in greater pain, in greater need, or in greater neglect than that large group of women whose husbands have not yet joined them in their faith."[10] We need now to see what effect this pain is having on people who have to suffer it constantly.

CHAPTER TWO

How Does This Affect You?

D o you feel that you are in a situation where you cannot win and that you are trapped in circumstances which you would never deliberately have chosen? Both God and your husband mean a lot to you. They both receive your love, but do they seem to be diametrically opposed to one another? No doubt you sometimes wonder where it will all end and how you will cope in the meantime. Perhaps you question whether or not you have the strength needed to carry on.

If such thoughts and questions pass through your mind, then you are alert to the fact that your situation is potentially harmful to you, your husband, and your family. This would be true whatever the bone of contention was between you and your husband. When the area of disagreement is something as deep as personal faith, however, there are perils lurking ahead of you that could have a particularly destructive effect on your life and the lives of others close to you.

This chapter is intended to make some of these perils clear. It does not suggest that all the problems discussed will become yours, but it does identify what kind of problems and dangers commonly befall wives in your situation.

YOUR SPIRITUAL GROWTH CAN BE STUNTED

People react differently when they are under heavy pressure. Some draw on hidden reserves, whether physical, mental or spiritual, and fight back. Others begin to crumble when pressures build up. Demas was standing firm for the Lord when Paul referred to him in Colossians 4:14, but by the time Paul wrote to Timothy for the second time, he had deserted him (2 Tm 4:10). It appears that he did so because "he loved this world."

Some wives with unconverted husbands find their faith suffers because of the pressure they have to endure. Sue is having "very hard times" at home because she trusts in Jesus, and feels that she is at a standstill as a Christian. Anne's husband accepts her faith as part of her even though he does not share it. She says, "The main problem is that I feel almost 'held back' by him as there are many things that I feel I should be doing, but don't do, because I am conscious of his opinions and the fact that I will be away from him when our time together is already limited. In a way I'm torn between God and him."

Some Christian wives feel they must try to steer a middle course at home, but this inevitably has its effects on their spiritual lives. This is Janice's situation. Her husband's background is verydifferent from her own. She has problems with the TV programs and videos shown in the family home, which contain bad language and sex. According to Janice, her husband regards sex "as the highlight of his life." In these circumstances she says that she "tries to compromise with all these problems without being too prim and proper," but the pressure takes its toll on her relationship with God.

THE GAP BETWEEN YOU AND YOUR
PARTNER MAY BE HIGHLIGHTED

As we saw earlier, Christian wives in these circumstances often feel torn between their unbelieving husbands and God. They feel that their faith separates them from their husbands. The sad thing is that things may not improve, at least not in the short term.

The apostle Paul taught that Christians should not marry unbelievers. His reasoning was simple and he explained it in a series of questions. "For what do righteousness and wickedness have in common? Or what fellowship can light have with darkness? What harmony is there between Christ and Belial? What does a believer have in common with an unbeliever? What agreement is there between the temple of God and idols?" (2 Cor 6:14-16).

Whether we like it or not, there is a gap between every born-again Christian and those who do not believe in Christ. To quote Paul,

> We have been justified through faith, we have peace with God through our Lord Jesus Christ, through whom we have gained access by faith into this grace in which we now stand. And we rejoice in the hope of the glory of God.
> **Romans 5:1-2**

God's gifts of forgiveness, eternal life, and the Holy Spirit bring about a remarkable transformation in the lives of those who receive them. This inevitably distinguishes them from those whose lives have not yet been touched by God.

Marion reports on the relationship she has with her husband since she became a Christian: "Instead of bringing us closer together it has made a gap. I am unable to share my faith with him. More and more we go our separate ways, spending less time together. I pray a lot about this situation, which helps. But I get very upset at times when I see how far apart we have become." This gap exists while a married couple remains spiritually divided.

YOU MAY FIND IT HARD TO
REMAIN PART OF THE CHURCH

In an earlier book, *The Sheep That Got Away*, I reported that 10 percent of those surveyed stopped attending church because of domestic tensions.[1] This is tragic but understandable. Constant and unrelenting pressure wears us down and there is only so much that anyone can take.

Sometimes, pressure at home has the effect of forcing a Christian wife to break links with her church, or at least to lessen them. Alison is having to do this. "I have had to accept his unwillingness to become involved with the church, and have cut back on the time I spend on church activities. I am a Sunday school secretary, but I attend church services irregularly as I feel I have to spend time with my family on Sundays."

The same can result if a Christian wife feels isolated and alienated at church too often or for too long. If she feels estranged within the fellowship and finds that no one comes close when she needs support most, she may conclude that she will lose very little by leaving altogether.

YOU COULD BE LURED TO MARITAL INFIDELITY

When a Christian wife discovers how rich her relationships with the Lord and other believers at church can be, she may reevaluate her relationship with her husband. She may realize how much harder it is to relate to him than to her friends at church. Her marriage may feel empty and lacking meaning and depth. She may feel isolated at home.

Ruth explains how tempting infidelity can be. "The infatuation always starts off after you have had an argument, when your husband 'doesn't understand' you, or you can't talk to him. In walks Mr. Perfect and you see him through your rose-colored glasses. He's always a religious man, someone who knows Jesus personally and is making a stand for him. He's someone who listens to you when you talk about spiritual things and who you feel meets your spiritual and emotional needs."

This can be a point of extreme danger. Linda Davis highlights what can happen:

Satan uses many fiery darts to tempt women into infidelity, but loneliness is probably chief among them. The wife of an unbeliever has a spiritual hunger for a Christian mate that can cause her to ache with loneliness even when her husband is sitting right next to her.[2]

The Bible not only forbids adultery in the Ten Commandments (Ex 20:14), but reveals the anger and pain that God feels when his children on earth sin in this way (2 Sm 11-12). The illicit affair may appeal strongly to our emotions because of our sensed need for a spiritual soulmate, but this course of action is guaranteed to bring more grief than fulfillment in the long term. Not only does it mean disobeying God and breaking our marriage vows, but our actions are likely to cause deep pain in our family and church. We will also ruin our witness for Christ.

Mercifully, Ruth can see what happens when Mr. Perfect appears. "We are dealing with the devil here, a liar and the father of lies," she says. "You see, the 'other man' syndrome is the easy option, the easy way out. You think, 'Why bother; let's call it quits and start again. If only you'd waited. This person would have been the right one for you.' Even harboring secret thoughts cannot continue because God knows of them, and that's why they must stop. Confession is part of the process of walking away from it. Not confession to your husband, because that would hurt him too much and ruin your marriage. Rather, confession to a trustworthy friend or, if that's not possible, just between you and God."

YOU MAY BE PERMANENTLY UNHAPPY

The Bible teaches that when a person becomes a Christian, God releases his Holy Spirit to them (Acts 2:38). The apostle Paul wrote that among the fruit of the Spirit is "joy" (Gal 5:22). It is God's plan that every believer should experience an inner joy through believing in Jesus and knowing him. This is easy to describe, but not necessarily easy to reconcile with the continuous pain experienced by Christians whose marriage partners do not believe.

As quoted above, when Paul presented his teaching about marriage to the Christians at Corinth, he asked "What fellowship can light have with darkness?... What does a believer have in common with an unbeliever?" (2 Cor 6:14-15). He knew that there is a sense in which two people become incompatible once one of them comes to faith in Christ. This will almost inevitably lead to misunderstanding and conflict between them if the believer is serious about living for Jesus.

One of the sad (and regrettable) consequences of this is that a marriage that was previously happy and stable can degenerate once one partner becomes a Christian. Both parties find the marriage less happy and more tense because now they have different priorities in life. For Margaret it means being thoroughly misunderstood. "My husband has a great deal of hate for the church and the fact that I love someone else more than him. He won't accept that my love of God is different than my love for him and that, in fact, it should help our marriage, not hinder it."

Irene expresses her difficulties in a more practical way. She says, "Before... I used to go to the bar with my husband a lot. Now I don't want to go... anymore. I find the atmosphere noisy and smoky, the opposite of what I enjoy." There are no easy answers to problems like these, and the Christian may have to continue to carry this pain.

YOUR MARRIAGE COULD BREAK DOWN

While many marriages can be sustained when just one of the partners is a Christian, others cannot.

Paul was aware of the problems that arise in these circumstances; they had surfaced in the Corinthian church. In his teaching his main aim is to keep marriages together, although he knows that some may well disintegrate. He provides clear guidelines:

> If any brother has a wife who is not a believer and she is willing to live with him, he must not divorce her. And if a woman has a husband who is not a believer and he is willing to live with her, she must not divorce him.
>
> **1 Corinthians 7:12-13**

Sometimes the unbelieving partner cannot stand it any longer. Perhaps the spouse, who has recently come to faith, has now become so different that it feels like being married to a stranger. Of course, it is good if the new convert has become more Christlike, but it can nevertheless be quite a shock to the unbelieving spouse.

Sometimes, however, it is the change in lifestyle which the partner notices first. When a previously home-loving spouse rushes out to church events night after night, it is disruptive and threatening; the normal pattern of life has been turned upside down. If the new Christian fails to heed direct warnings or even threats, the unbeliever may feel that the only thing left to do is to leave. Although reconciliation is possible once a couple has separated informally, many relationships deteriorate from this point, and it may not be long before the formal processes are begun which ultimately lead to either a legal separation or divorce.

Liz has been threatened with both. "My husband has a lot of jealousy and resentment toward my commitment to Jesus. He feels rejected. He never bothered about my sporadic and occasional churchgoing in the past because it wasn't serious and wasn't a threat to him. Now because he sees my dedication to the Lord as serious, he can't cope with it and lashes out whenever he can. He has used threats that include separation and divorce, and even physical violence at times. He used to phone up some of my pastors when he was drunk and took particular delight in using foul language toward the female pastor, being abusive for an hour or more. He now resorts to verbal abuse and to refusing to listen to anything of a 'religious' nature."

Sadly, Stephanie is now separated from her husband. Her husband's values were at odds with her own. "He values ambition, success, independence, and putting himself first. He takes the children to bars. Before we separated we had three main problem areas. He hated me reading the Bible and singing and playing Christian songs; he hated all Christians and didn't like them in the house; on Sundays he wanted the kids at home with him, while I wanted them at church with me."

YOUR CHILDREN MAY BE AFFECTED

It is well recognized that to become stable and self-confident adults, children need plenty of love and security in their childhood years.

The operative factor is the parent, and the parent's behavior, and the two parents' inter-relationship as perceived by the child. It is this that the child takes in, and imitates or reacts against, and it is this also that the child uses in a hundred ways in the personal process of self-development.[3]

The realization that disagreements in the home about faith and church are having an adverse effect on the children can come as a nasty shock to parents who try very hard to take their responsibilities seriously. Some of us find it easy to put our heads in the sand, deny that we have a serious problem, and carry on as before, hoping for the best. Even well-meaning parents do this at times, and if problems over faith arise in a marriage, we may be oblivious to the probable long-term effects on the children.

All sorts of difficulties arise in practice, as four wives explain. Sophie says that both she and her husband agreed that their children should go to Sunday school, but when she answers their questions at home, her husband laughs. She is not sure what the children make of it, but they have asked, "Why doesn't Daddy love Jesus?"

Jill's husband runs a junior soccer team whose games are always on Sunday mornings. "Our son plays on this team, and so doesn't come to church. This means the 'boys' go to soccer and the 'girls' go to church."

Joanne's husband mocks her in front of their son about going to church, and has also "tried to tempt him with a better offer than church, for example staying home with Daddy and playing on the go-cart."

Deborah is worried for her teenagers because her husband influences them about worldly things. "He's always telling stories in front of them about the fun he's had when drunk. I'm worried that they will get into drink, drugs, and sleeping around."

YOU MAY FEEL SPIRITUALLY DEPRIVED

Christian wives whose husbands do not share their faith notice what they miss out on. They know that they cannot get to church or to their local small group every week. They are aware that the wives with Christian husbands make plans early on to go to major church events. They know that they miss out because their husband simply will not go.

It is easy to feel sorry for ourselves when we do not have the freedom that others seem to enjoy and take for granted. Yet we must never forget that Christianity is a faith rooted in sacrifice. The Father sacrificed his Son, Jesus sacrificed his life, and the apostle Paul and other early Christian leaders sacrificed their freedom for those who had not heard the gospel.

Jesus made it clear that Christian discipleship would involve pain and deprivation, but God so often compensates us in other ways when we suffer for his sake. It is as we graciously accept sacrifice that we have another opportunity to move forward in our Christian lives. God seems to bless our positive attitude and lack of resentment.

YOUR CHURCH MAY MAKE THINGS HARDER

Ideally, those who are part of a local church will never deliberately make life more difficult for others in the fellowship. Sadly, some wives whose husbands are not Christians feel that their church has not made it any easier for their mates to find Christ.

Catherine says that the first time her husband went to church, "they tried to register him for the church men's organization! Then the first time we took our foster son, we had verbal abuse from two old ladies who said that he had given them a headache." Stephanie, already upset that no men in the church have bothered to befriend her husband, tells of one church member's wedding when all non-Christian husbands were excluded. "That's *really* bad," she says.

Gillian recalls, "A number of years ago we went for a meal with a Christian couple. The husband at the time was very critical of the church of which we were members and spent much of the evening finding fault with it. On returning home my husband commented that he thought Christians were supposed to live in harmony."

Valerie's experience was different. "When I first started going to church, someone knocked on our door to visit us. My husband was really annoyed because he felt we were being pressured."

Margaret's problems arose when, "a few years ago, our church had a big split and half the congregation followed the minister and set up a new fellowship. It was a bitter split and my husband relished every bit of the gossip he could get (not from me, which caused problems because he said I was keeping secrets from him)."

At times like this we realize how imperfect Christians and churches still are. The communities that Jesus intended should draw others to him sometimes accomplish the opposite. For the Christian wife, this can be a source of extreme frustration and may very easily lead to anger and resentment. Sometimes the positive effect of years of gentle witnessing at home can be negated in a moment. When this happens she has only God to fall back on.

We need to be honest. Being married to a husband who does not share your faith is not easy. The effects on you, him, and your family can be difficult to cope with. You may have pain, hurt, and hardship to bear.

Now we need to move on from discussing how tough it can be, to discovering how much help God can give you.

CHAPTER THREE

How Can God Help You?

Having a partner who does not share your faith can be very hard. Pain is probably commonplace in your life. The Bible never promises believers that life on earth will be easy, and Christians can have as tough a time as anyone else, but they have a distinct advantage over those with no personal faith. God's strength and help can make a vast difference in the hard times.

In this chapter we will explore the variety of ways in which God can help us when life is painful. He has a wonderful capacity to minister directly to the needs that we have.

GOD WILL ALWAYS LISTEN TO YOU

Whereas human friends can be unavailable when we need them most, we encounter no such problems when, possibly in the thick of a crisis, we call on God for help. Unlike Baal, god of the Canaanites, whom Elijah suggested may have been too busy, traveling, or asleep (1 Kgs 18:27), our God is always accessible to those who trust him.

The Bible encourages us to call on God whenever we need him. The writer of Psalm 30, for instance, speaks of being in "the depths" and "the grave" and feeling that God had hidden his face from him. Yet when he called to God for help, God heard and healed him and turned his "wailing into dancing" and clothed him "with joy." The message is clear: God will hear our cries and take our predicament seriously whenever we realize that we cannot handle our problems alone and therefore put our trust in him.

When life at home or in church is difficult to handle because you are having to cope alone, God will be there to listen to you. You can have the same confidence about this as the psalmist who wrote, "The Lord will hear when I call to him" (Ps 4:3).

GOD WILL SHARE YOUR PAIN

Life at home can be difficult when husband and wife are at odds over an important issue. Especially when the fighting is over our Christian faith, we need to remember that God is there with us and for us. Not only can we pour out our anger, frustration, pain, and hurt to him, but he can reassure us of his understanding, love, and care (1 Pt 5:7). Another bonus is that whereas we may need to be discreet when telling other people of our situation, we can be both honest and direct with God. This in itself can be wonderfully liberating.

The example of the psalmists is that they were very honest with God as they poured out their problems. "Turn to me and be gracious to me, for I am lonely and afflicted. The troubles of my heart have multiplied; free me from my anguish" (Ps 25:16-17). "Hear, O Lord, and answer me, for I am poor and needy. Guard my life, for I am devoted to you. You are my God; save your servant who trusts in you" (Ps 86:1-2).

Many people have proved the love and faithfulness of God once they have poured out their pain and frustration to him. Helen's experience is that God helps her. She says, "Although I find I can discuss or mention faith more and more in conversation, my husband likes me to keep a low profile. He says he has no objection to my attending church, but does not want me to 'get involved.' He absolutely forbade me to give out leaflets when a special choir came to our church, but I know six people came through opportunities I took and 'chance' meetings I had without me needing to break a promise. God had his way!" What matters for you too is that God can give you the resources you need to cope with your own situation.

GOD WILL ENCOURAGE YOU

The Bible shows us that God understands the sadness that is common among wives whose husbands do not share their faith. The reason for this is simple: God also experiences this emotion. This is particularly evident in Hosea's prophecy, where God laments the way that his chosen Jewish people (sometimes called "Ephraim" in this passage) have deserted him despite all he has done for them.

> When Israel was a child, I loved him, and out of Egypt I called my son. But the more I called Israel, the further they went from me. They sacrificed to the Baals and they burned incense to images. It was I who taught Ephraim to walk, taking them by the arms; but they did not realize it was I who healed them..... How can I give you up, Ephraim? How can I hand you over, Israel? How can I treat you like Admah? How can I make you like Zeboiim? My heart is changed within me; all my compassion is aroused.
>
> **Hosea 11:1-3, 8**

Jesus experienced sadness during his ministry. One of the Twelve, Judas Iscariot, agreed to betray him in exchange for financial gain (Mt 26:14-16). When Jesus was arrested, all the disciples "deserted him and fled" (Mt 26:56), while Simon Peter denied knowing him three times (Mt 26:69-75).

God understands when we are saddened because our circumstances are less than ideal and particularly when they involve the person on earth who means the most to us. Moreover, he has a special ministry to us. Many centuries before Jesus came, Isaiah spoke some words of prophecy which Jesus later fulfilled and related to himself. "The Spirit of the Sovereign Lord is on me, because the Lord has anointed me to preach good news to the poor. He has sent me to bind up the broken-hearted" (Is 61:1, cf Lk 4:18).

GOD WILL STRENGTHEN YOU

When we cannot find a human solution to our problems, God's resources can make a world of difference. Paul was troubled with "a thorn in my flesh," which he also describes as "a messenger of Satan" and which he believed was there "to torment me" (2 Cor 12:7). It was as he tried to cope with this that he learned that God's "power is made perfect in weakness" (2 Cor 12:9). Indeed, he goes on to say that he "delights" in having problems and hardships, "For when I am weak, then I am strong" (2 Cor 12:10).

You may be able to draw reassurance from the many testimonies in the Bible that pay tribute to God's love and support in demanding times. He promised Joshua his presence when he became the leader of the Israelites (Josh 1:5), and Gideon his resources as he led God's people into battle (Jgs 6:16). In both cases he kept his word. The writer of Psalm 28 testifies that "the Lord is my strength" and "the strength of his people." Much later the apostle Peter, who went through many demanding situations as he served his Master, wrote to bring encouragement to his readers. He told them that God "will... make you strong, firm, and steadfast" (1 Pt 5:10), something he could only say with such confidence if he himself had experienced it.

One wife told me how bad things were soon after she came

to faith in Christ. Her husband drank heavily and, on occasions, after drinking bouts, attacked her both verbally and physically. He was very vicious, she recalled, and she was frightened. At that time she coped very poorly and used to get very upset over the terrible abuse. This no longer happens, although she still gets attacked verbally if he does not agree with some aspect of her Christian life. She testifies to the way that God is very much more real to her now and his peace is a great help.

GOD WILL HELP YOU TO KEEP PRAYING

The best thing you can do for your husband is to pray for him, not occasionally, but regularly and consistently. You may not find this easy, especially if he is antagonistic toward God, your faith, and your church. It may seem more natural for you to divide your mind and emotions in half so that you love him with one part of you, and love God with another. The message you receive from your husband is clear: he is hostile toward God, or at least unimpressed and unconvinced.

God is not in the least hostile toward him; on the contrary, God loves him. God is eager to work in his life if only he could break through. You can pray that this will happen in due course. Be aware, though, that it may not be easy to keep praying if you do not see anything obvious changing. At times like this all you can do is trust God.

Linda has been doing this and has found it works. "I pray every day for my husband and son and place them in God's hands," she says. "He does answer prayer. A counselor in our church told me to hold my husband's hand and then with the other hand hold Jesus' hand and then pray that through me the Holy Spirit would soften his heart and change him. I have been doing this every night in bed and there has been a big change. He has started to listen to me, he is softer and now actually encourages me to attend meetings."

Other Christian wives find that, as they pray, something positive happens in *them*. Their own faith in God expands and their spiritual life deepens. This is Julie's experience. She says that a lot of people pray for her husband and therefore she finds it easier to feel that "it is under God's control. I trust his timing."

Karen is sure that her constant praying is benefiting her own spiritual life, even though her husband has not yet responded. "I realize that I cannot want him saved more than my Lord Jesus does. I may still be praying without effect, through lack of understanding, but I am learning more about prayer every day," she says. With encouragements like this, you will more easily be able to keep praying during difficult times.

GOD WILL HELP YOU LISTEN FOR HIM

If things at home are at their worst and you keep hearing words and attitudes of condemnation against God, Christianity, and the church, it is not easy to listen for the voice of God in that same environment. A survey conducted by *Christian Family* and Maranatha Ministries showed that 12 percent of husbands became increasingly hostile after their wives became Christians.[1] This hostility was expressed verbally and physically. When under attack, listening for God's voice may seem less important than just surviving. One wife told me that her husband has recently reverted to blaspheming if he is angry with her. He admits he does it to hurt her. She says, "My biggest coping mechanism is prayer."

Like Elijah, we need to hear the "gentle whisper" of God's voice (1 Kgs 19:12) to give us reassurance for the present and future. Unless we give God the chance to speak, we will not know what he has to say to us. Continuing to devote time to prayer and reading the Bible is of great importance, whether we feel like it or not. Meeting with other Christians in a small group as well as at church is important too, if we can make time for it. We need to hear from God. Kathleen's testimony is, "As long as I'm listening to what God is saying, I have peace."[2]

In practice, however, this is not always easy. Sue tells how her husband used to interrupt her during her prayer time. "I don't know if he knew he was doing it or not," she says, "so now I try to have my prayer time when I know he will not interrupt, like when he's in the bathroom or taking a shower."

GOD WILL HELP YOU TO MAINTAIN YOUR WITNESS

It is easier for some wives to witness openly about their faith at home than for others. Julie is taking it slowly. "I talk naturally about God as though he's a friend with whom I've just had coffee. I choose significant moments in everyday situations to project God's ways and blessings to him," she says. Not all wives find it as straightforward as this.

Hilary has been married for twenty-two years. Her husband feels that Christians, and especially Christian men, are weak and gullible. She says, "I pray a lot, love him a lot, and keep to the verses the Lord gave me when I first became a Christian." These are Peter's words: "Wives... be submissive to your husbands so that, if any of them do not believe the word, they may be won over without words by the behavior of their wives, when they see the purity and reverence of your lives" (1 Pt 3:1-2).

Erica learned the hard way how to maintain a quiet witness. She recalls,

In the first few years after being born-again and finding a personal relationship with the Lord, I used opportunities when my husband was feeling low to tell him how Jesus had changed my life completely and that this was for him too. But any attempts to direct him to God made him angry. I used to leave books around and do and say things that I now see as manipulation, because of what I wanted for him. Now I just love and understand him as much as possible and try to be an obedient wife, except in any instance of going against God's will. When he asks questions I try to answer honestly, simply, and *briefly*. A lovely counselor friend advised me to "watch, pray, and sometimes weep."

When the witnessing seems to be having no effect, we need a fresh vision of what God can do. He can give us this as we read the Bible, hear it preached, study it alone or with others, and as we meet with fellow believers in worship. What he shares is the reassurance that it is still worthwhile to witness at home, even though your husband gives no indication yet of turning to Christ. The Bible tells us that witnessing for God is never wasted (Is 55:11).

GOD WILL GIVE YOU PATIENCE

Every human being on earth is at a measurable point of contact with God. As Engel's Scale shows (see chart, page 50), some people are hardly aware of the existence of God, if at all.[3] Your husband may be somewhere in the -10 to -5 range. The purpose of this chart is to show that, generally, people have to progress through a number of stages of awareness and understanding before they are ready to make a commitment of their life to Jesus. It is important to understand this. The reality is that it is rare for people to commit their lives to Jesus out of the blue, although it does happen occasionally. They usually only do so following a period of serious exploration, when they feel ready.

Perhaps you can estimate how near or far your partner is from God at present, although you need to accept that you may be wrong! Recognizing that men are not always the best verbal communicators of their feelings, you must realize that even you may be in the dark. How should you respond, then, if you sense he is fairly low on the scale and still a long way from God? My first suggestion is that you accept things as they are, even though you are praying for changes. Understand, as we have already said, that you cannot make him a Christian anyway and that, at best, you have a small part to play in encouraging him to make an exploratory journey toward personal faith in Christ.

If you accept that your husband is unlikely to become a Christian right away, God will give you his peace if you talk with him about it in prayer. God has a wonderful ability to reassure us even when external circumstances are not ideal. This is what Linda Davis experienced when her husband, after many years of praying and hoping, still did not respond to Christ.

I, too, eventually learned the secret of acceptance with joy in the middle of my desert experience. I'm sure it was born not so much out of Christian maturity as human desperation. I was sick of being miserable. Something inside me said, "Enough already! I'm tired of waiting to be happy. If my husband doesn't get saved until he is ninety-nine years old, just look at all the years I will have wasted being miserable about it. This is my life, and I'm not going to waste any more of it being unhappy about something I have no power to change. I'm just going to have to accept what I can't change and be happy in spite of it!" I finally realized the absurdity of living with the attitude, "Someday my husband will get saved, and then I'll be happy." It finally dawned on me that life is not made up of "somedays" but of thousands of "todays." If I wanted to enjoy my life— ever—I had to enjoy it and be happy *today*—regardless of circumstances and no matter what my husband's spiritual condition.[4]

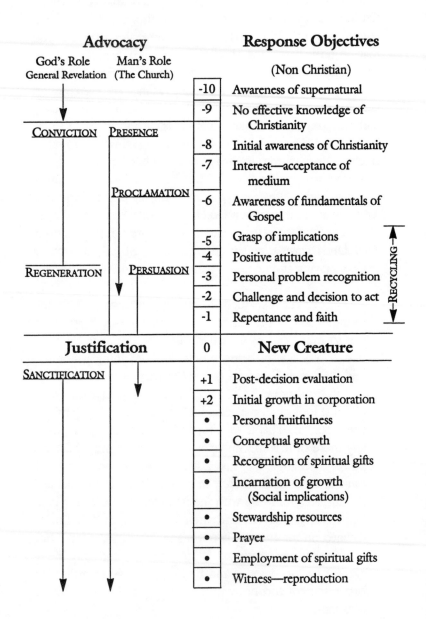

Advocacy			Response Objectives
God's Role General Revelation	Man's Role (The Church)		(Non Christian)
		-10	Awareness of supernatural
		-9	No effective knowledge of Christianity
CONVICTION	PRESENCE	-8	Initial awareness of Christianity
		-7	Interest—acceptance of medium
	PROCLAMATION	-6	Awareness of fundamentals of Gospel
		-5	Grasp of implications
		-4	Positive attitude
REGENERATION	PERSUASION	-3	Personal problem recognition
		-2	Challenge and decision to act
		-1	Repentance and faith
Justification		0	**New Creature**
SANCTIFICATION		+1	Post-decision evaluation
		+2	Initial growth in corporation
		•	Personal fruitfulness
		•	Conceptual growth
		•	Recognition of spiritual gifts
		•	Incarnation of growth (Social implications)
		•	Stewardship resources
		•	Prayer
		•	Employment of spiritual gifts
		•	Witness—reproduction

RECYCLING

GOD WILL HELP YOU BREAK FREE FROM GUILT

Christians often have a greater sensitivity about guilt than most other people and usually this is good. This sensitivity is possibly because our faith is rooted in a God who is righteous and moral. When we sin, the Holy Spirit convicts us, and when we repent, trusting in the blood of Christ shed for us on the cross, God forgives us.

Jackie and her fiance agonized for four years before getting married. He was a non-observant Jew, she was a Christian who had been converted at college. After their wedding, she had to seek prayer counseling at her church. Among other things, she "received crucial help to confess, be cleansed and freed from guilt for disobeying 2 Corinthians 6:14, 'Do not be yoked together with unbelievers.'"

Hazel's experience was similar:

We moved to our present church when we married and at that point I knew I had disobeyed God. I went to church because I felt guilty before God. I was also depressed, mainly because I had deliberately disobeyed God's Word. It was through fellowship with other members of the church that I eventually realized that God would forgive me for marrying a "non-Christian" if I asked him to. A great burden was lifted from me. Now my husband and I are both given lots of encouragement. We have made good friends and my husband has been encouraged to play football and squash with members of our church.

Some Christian wives experience a false kind of guilt that makes them suffer inner pain and torment until they are released from it. One unhelpful (and utterly false) doctrine that encourages this guilt is one that teaches that, whenever things do not go well in a Christian's life, it is because they have sinned and therefore God is angry with them. When a

Christian wife whose husband does not share her faith experiences hard and painful times, she may (if she believes this) wrongly conclude that she has committed serious sins and is now paying the price for them. She may believe that God is punishing her in order to force her to greater obedience and dedication in the future.

While God *may* be doing this, in most cases he is not. The main problem is that she has absorbed faulty teaching. The Bible teaches us about God's justice, but also of his patience. When Christians sin, God does not rush to punish them with a big stick, but sends his Holy Spirit to show them their error. Only when this gentle and loving approach fails to get through over a period of time does God consider other alternatives. The Jewish people refused to respond to God's patient but firm ministry over a period of centuries. Eventually, God allowed them to be taken into exile in Babylon.

There are simple ways of discerning whether we are truly guilty before God, or carrying imagined guilt that we are imposing on ourselves. When God convicts us of sin, he tells us clearly and precisely what it is that we have done that has offended him. Satan's approach is different. He swamps us with a general feeling of inadequacy and failure, but we cannot identify anything specific that we have done wrong. If we check this with Christian friends, they should be able to help us clarify whether our guilt feelings are genuine (in which case we need to respond to God's call for repentance) or false (in which case we need to tell Satan to go away). We need to be free of guilt feelings if we are to serve God faithfully.

GOD WILL BUILD YOUR FAITH

Your situation at home may be demanding and the relationship between you and your partner strained and causing you both distress. You are aware that the current situation is grim and the future prognosis is bleak. What are you to do as a believer, especially because you are eager to have not just a good marriage, but a Christian partner too?

The answer is that a great deal depends on your general attitude, the depth of commitment to your marriage vows, and your level of faith in God. You may have reached the stage where you are wondering if it is worth trying any longer. Maybe your level of despair is so deep that it would take a lot to persuade you even to contemplate staying with your husband long-term. Humanly, your relationship appears to be over.

Giving up on the relationship because it is unhappy and seems unproductive may not be so easy if you are a Christian. While anyone, of course, can legally separate and divorce, those who acknowledge God and his Word as a higher authority may have problems doing either—unless, of course, they or their children are in danger.

God says that marriage is for life (Mt 19:4-6), and his view of the disintegration of marriage is made very clear in his words in Malachi 2:16, "I hate divorce" (although here he is speaking of the unfaithfulness of his chosen people who broke the covenant established when Moses was their leader; see Exodus 24:7-8). Jesus emphasized in Matthew 19:8-9 that to be able to divorce was a concession God allowed Moses to grant because of human weakness. He also made it clear that in God's sight there is no automatic right to remarry after divorce. This provision is only for those whose marriage has crumbled after their partner has betrayed them by committing adultery.

While Western society as a whole takes marriage vows less and less seriously, and has no qualms about terminating unloving and unfulfilling marriages, the matter is not this simple for Christians. What should a Christian wife do if the prospects of finding happiness and contentment with her unbelieving husband are slender?

She may have to decide between upholding and obeying God's Word and doing what humanly may seem to be the obvious and easier option of allowing the marriage to continue going downhill, possibly toward divorce. In 1 Corinthians 7 Paul teaches the Christians in Corinth who are married to unbelievers that so long as their partner will live with them, the believer must not initiate divorce (v 12-13). He explains why in verse 14. So long as they live together, even if unhappily, the Christian partner can gently influence the other by living a godly life. This leaves the door open for God to work through the Christian partner if and when the unbeliever is ready.

For a Christian to do this demands tremendous dedication to God because he or she would be doing it primarily for him. This, though, is when God's power, love, strength, and hope can flow most freely. When followers of Jesus make sacrificial decisions out of obedience to him, God will never desert them. Lawrence Crabb advocates this course of action in these circumstances.

> If we remain faithful to God, pouring out our emotions before Him, renewing our commitment to seek Him, trusting Him to guide us in our responses, then He will sustain us through our trials and provide rich fellowship with Him. There is reason to go on. There is hope. God's grace is sufficient.
>
> Perhaps your spouse will not join you on the path to oneness. But you can maintain your commitment—first to obey God and then to minister to your spouse through each opportunity that arises. The result will *possibly* be a better marriage (and in many cases *probably*). The result will *surely* be a new level of spiritual maturity and fellowship with Christ for you.[5]

GOD WILL ANSWER YOUR PRAYERS

God makes it clear to us in the Bible that he wants human beings to share a relationship with him. Once established, this relationship is kept alive through prayer, with Christians having the opportunity to bring their intercessions directly to God. While some prayers are answered without much delay, many are not and God tests the extent of our faith by seeing if we persevere by continuing to ask (Lk 11:5-8). One thing is certain: God answers every prayer from his children. To some he says "yes," to others "no," to others "wait." If, then, you are praying about your situation as a Christian when your partner does not yet believe, how may God respond?

When you pray, perhaps you ask for your husband to come to trust Jesus Christ. In that case, he just might! The Bible teaches that prayer works! God responded to the prayers of the Jerusalem church and freed Peter from jail just before he was due to be executed (Acts 12:1-17). Jesus explained that his own power came "by prayer" (Mk 9:29). God responds when his children pray and simply trust him (Mt 7:7-11).

Do not underestimate what happens when you pray for your partner regularly. God responds to your faith and to your desire that your husband should receive the best gift ever offered to human beings. He is glad that you are praying in line with his will (1 Tm 2:3-4) and releases spiritual power that does two things. First, it holds back the powers of darkness that have some kind of grip on your husband. This allows him to become more open and responsive to spiritual issues, if he is willing to. Second, God works in his life by the Holy Spirit to give him spiritual insight—again, if he is open to be shown. We must not lose sight of this truth. The Bible teaches clearly that no one becomes a Christian through using human faculties alone, for God personally reveals his truth to us (1 Cor 2:10) and it is then that we can respond.

While we can pray and God can work, no one becomes a

follower of Jesus unless and until they make a personal response to God of their own free will. I could not make you become a Christian, nor you me. I personally responded to God at a camp in Sussex, England, when I was fourteen, and presumably you have done something similar. No one, apart from your husband, can decide how he should respond to the love of God as seen in Jesus Christ.

Linda Davis tells the story of Pat who believed for over twenty years that her husband would be converted. Even when her husband was diagnosed as having terminal cancer and his physical condition declined monthly, she still trusted God to save him and kept praying. One day God spoke to her and said, "I'll leave no stone unturned, but it is your husband's decision."[6] You cannot make him love God, but you can pray for him. In chapter five we will discuss some practical things you can do alongside your praying.

GOD WILL GIVE YOU ANOTHER FAMILY

Finally, let us consider the situation of a wife whose marriage does not provide the love, mutual friendship, and encouragement that she had hoped for and expected, especially if part of what divides them is her Christian faith. In these circumstances, where better for her needs to be met than in the church?

Paul alludes to the church as God's family (1 Tm 3:5). While this kind of family cannot provide twenty-four-hour-a-day support, it can help in various ways to take the edge off the pain. Where a church provides support ministry for those with such needs, they must take care that it does not threaten the situation back home and possibly make it worse. Rather, it should be seen as God's loving provision through his family.

This can be God's way of investing in one of his children with a particular need, so that she can continue to give herself to her marriage. God's desire is to bring the marriage back to life. By meeting the needs of one partner through a church family, both husband and wife are sustained and helped through a tough time.

In this chapter I have highlighted a number of different ways in which God can help you, but before we move on to think about things from your husband's perspective, we will restate what we have considered: Whatever the circumstances you are in, God loves you, has not forgotten you, and is committed to helping you in any number of different ways. He is eager that you should be able to experience his love for you—even if times are hard.

PART TWO

All About Your Husband

CHAPTER FOUR

What Is Your Husband Going Through?

It is likely that it is not just you who finds it difficult coping at home; your husband probably does too. If the differences that exist between you because of your faith in God cause you to struggle, how do you think he reacts? He may not have told you, so in this chapter we will try to get inside the mind and emotions of a husband whose wife has a faith that he does not share.

Let us begin by recognizing that men and women are quite different emotionally and practically, and function differently in relationships. In order to understand something of what goes on, particularly in romantic relationships, we will note differences in the way the two sexes tick.

Many women enjoy conversation because it enables them to build connections with others and develop a sense of intimacy with them. Men, however, often use conversations to demonstrate their independence and status. They do not seem to find it so easy to open up and talk about personal, emotional, or intimate matters, and often relate best to other men when focusing on particular issues like business, sports, or politics. Men often find it hard to admit to feelings of inadequacy and do not appear to need a network of friends in the same way as women do.

This does not mean, however, that men prefer solitude and isolation. Jim Smith, a Christian evangelist, says that "men have a very strong herding instinct. They react to things together, discussing them and throwing in their opinion."[1] They also like a fight and a challenge, and tend to think they are cleverer than women and more capable at most things. Many women, believing this to be untrue, try to control men in order to prove that men are not superior. Women are widely recognized as being more intuitive and they tend to be more people-oriented, whereas men are more task-oriented. Finally, men have a capacity to compartmentalize their lives in a way women generally do not do, so women may see men as inconsistent because they can make decisions that seem incompatible, yet relate to different areas of their lives.

In the light of these substantial differences between the sexes, it is hardly surprising that there is misunderstanding in some marriages. A wide variety of issues become barriers between husbands and wives including, of course, the faith of one that the other does not share.

In this chapter we will look at some of the many ways that a husband may respond when his wife goes to church (perhaps with the children) and leaves him at home on a regular basis, both on Sunday and during the week. No two men, their wives or circumstances, are the same, so the most we can do is highlight certain recurring feelings that surface in men in this situation.

JEALOUSY

Marie was married to Bill and had only recently become a Christian. Bridget Hall, in telling their story, says that Marie "had found a deeper meaning to her life and many new friends with whom she wanted to spend her time." Bill, however, could not understand her enthusiasm about church. He "felt rather threatened by it and became jealous and suspicious."[2]

Malcolm feels the same way. Sally has been a Christian for three years and he has noticed the change in her, mostly for the better. Describing Sally, Gavin Wakefield reports that "her tongue is less vicious, and she doesn't seem so restless."[3] Yet she and Malcolm have problems at home. Instead of going out for the evening together once a week as they used to, she now goes off to a church group and spends the evening with people he hardly knows. The fact that they are nearly all women gives him some reassurance, but...

> underneath it all, Malcolm is somewhat jealous of Sally's new relationship with Jesus. Jesus seems to get in the way of their marriage, which he'd always thought was very close. Now he finds it hard to discuss things with Sally, and when they do it often leads to an argument.[4]

After Linda Davis' husband, Mark, had become a Christian, she asked him how he felt about their relationship when, for many years, she had believed and he had not. She says that his expression...

> saddened as he recaptured memories of the feelings he had experienced.... When a man's wife becomes a Christian, it's a whole different kind of threat. Suddenly she has a love relationship with someone he can't even see. He can't understand anything she tries to tell him about this new God she has come to know. All he knows is that she's in love with somebody else and he is jealous. Instead of remaining the first priority in her life as when they first got married, he has suddenly been demoted to number two after God.[5]

When any husband begins to get a message like this, it is hardly surprising if he feels jealous. He may also feel the same way if his wife has any protracted contact with other men at church. Ruth says, "A man from church phoned me and my husband answered. It was to give a message to two other

Christian friends who don't have a telephone. I spent a weekend trying to convince my husband I was not having an affair with this man."

Pauline says that the biggest problem between her and her husband is his jealousy. "He told me once that he would prefer me to have a boyfriend rather than God (because he could fight that)." Angela senses that her husband has become increasingly jealous recently because there is a part of her life in which he is not involved.

What is reassuring about the response of these husbands is that their jealousy demonstrates that they care a great deal about their wives.

HURT

Rejection is painful, and when we feel we have been ousted from a former position of privilege and respect, it hurts deeply. Mark Davis, having felt he was being "demoted," says that "the husband feels that he hasn't changed—*she* has. She has broken the marriage contract. In his eyes, she is being unfaithful."[6]

This message can be communicated all too easily by even the most well-meaning wife. Jill says that her husband admits that he is "a very moody and bad-tempered person." However, she also says that she remembers telling him many years ago that she "loved Jesus more than him because he brought us together and is the Lord of all." We can only wonder if he has been deeply hurt by this, even if his wife meant no harm when she said it.

While the situation is very different from that in which the wife has an affair with another man, in the eyes of her husband it is not that different. Whomever she is having a relationship with, the fact is that he has become apparently less important to her than he was before. Women do not tend to see it this way at all, certainly not Margaret. She says, "My husband has a great deal of hate for the church and the fact that I love someone else more than him. He won't accept that my love of God is different from my love for him and that, in fact, it should help our marriage, not hinder it."

Some wives may be tempted to think that their husbands, usually tough and unable to communicate emotions, could never feel hurt in this kind of way. It is true that men do not divulge their feelings as easily or as often as women, but that does not mean they cannot and do not feel hurt. Your husband may not tell you, but he could be feeling rejected because you now have Jesus and your church to meet your spiritual needs, which he could not do for you.

Eleanor's husband probably felt emotionally wounded when he reacted to her baptism. She says, "When I was baptized he was irritable and hardly spoke to me for several weeks. He made me feel that I had done something wrong." When someone feels hurt, there is no certainty how they will respond.

PRESSURE

When a wife becomes a Christian, her husband may react in any number of ways. Neil did not have a problem when his wife found faith in Christ. "I believe that as a person my wife is entitled to do or believe in whatever she chooses," he said. His difficulty began to surface soon afterward. "When my wife first became a practicing Christian, I think she thought that I should follow suit and tried hard to get me to join in her praise." He did not want to do this.

Mark Davis experienced the same. After Linda became a Christian she started "pressuring him to love her God, too." This made him resentful. "It's worse than if, after my wife and I had gotten married, my mother-in-law moved in, and she and my wife took sides against me."[7]

The testimony of husbands suggests that Christian wives need to be careful not to make it harder for their husbands to find Christ by pressuring them too much. A man who feels threatened by pressure is likely to dig his heels in. Humanly, at least, this kind of tactic can make it much harder for him ever to come to Christ.

Mandy's husband has mixed feelings about the Christian faith. She says,

> He does believe in God and therefore believes he is a Christian, but as to having a personal relationship with the living Lord Jesus, that's quite a different matter. He's an independent, strong-minded, plain-speaking man. He's attracted to it, yet feels threatened by it. He keeps it at arm's length and can't cope with it being personal.

For Anne's husband, the threat is not so much Jesus directly, but the Body of Christ on earth. She reports, "I think he feels quite threatened by the church as an institution, as if they're going to subvert him."

UNEASINESS

Many couples begin married life with an established set of friends, some of whom are also married. Quite naturally, they spend time socializing and enjoying leisure time with these friends. Then one day the wife becomes a Christian, and not only does she begin a relationship with Jesus Christ, but the church suddenly becomes central in her social life too. She makes new friends there who become important to her, but they are not friends that she and her husband share. Sally's husband, Malcolm, has "met Margaret and some of the others once or twice, and they seem friendly enough,"[8] but he does not really see them as his sort of people.

This leaves a husband feeling uneasy that others have infiltrated his wife's life without his agreement, and he is not sure how to get her back for himself. Neither is he sure where it is all going to end. He may wonder if this could lead to the collapse of their marriage, because their relationship is being stretched too far.

EMOTIONAL SEPARATION

A couple that has been happy and content with each other may begin to sense emotional differences coming between them if one of them becomes a Christian. This is not necessarily because the other disapproves, but simply because of the changes taking place in the new believer's life.

Let us consider a situation where a husband has just become a Christian. He may be excited about his newfound faith and want to share it with others. Who better to start with than his wife at home? Linda Davis tells of such a man.

"I came home from work every night and started telling her about the Lord and why she must become a Christian," he said. "I made her sit and listen to me as I read the Bible. I refused to give in."[9]

The problem, to begin with, was that "she thought his 'religion' was foolish and embarrassing" and resisted all his hard-sell."[10] It became a battle of wills that he won in the end. This is not the point, however. Indoctrination, emotional pressure, and brute force are hardly the methods used by Jesus to win disciples. He explained his mission and calling, and then invited others to join him. If some left him, as John 6:66 recalls, he let them go. Jesus was not trying to recruit people unless they came willingly.

To act differently from Jesus is dangerous. Not only are we likely to get people to make so-called commitments to Christ for all the wrong reasons, but these people may also grow to resent the way we treated them. We only have to remember people who are pestered by insurance or window salesmen until they are worn down enough to give in and agree to a purchase. Afterward, in the cool light of day, they see more clearly. They know their resistance was attacked until the moment when the salesman could manipulate them.

It is humiliating to realize that someone has treated you in this way. A wife is in danger of driving a wedge between herself and her husband if she exerts unfair pressure on him. Such behavior can only harm relationships, even if it is being done for the best of motives. He may feel hurt which, if left to fester, can do irreparable harm to their marriage.

INDIFFERENCE

Some husbands, if their wives do not threaten them with a heavy-handed approach, may be quite happy to cooperate with them over their church attendance. They have no personal desire to have a faith of their own and may feel completely indifferent about Christianity, yet are prepared to support their partner.

In some ways Neil is such a husband. He sees himself as a "Christian person" and believes "that the church is a good thing for a lot of people if they wish to show their belief." Yet he is unconvinced that he should go. "I don't at this moment feel the need to prove my faith to other people or the way I lead my life," he says, while warmly supporting his wife as her faith grows.

CHALLENGE

Some husbands find themselves in a dilemma. They can see that their wives have genuinely changed since they became Christians and started going to church. One husband told his wife that he is well aware that she is different now, and certainly better to live with. The question he and other men have to face is why?

During my research I asked the participants if they thought that more women than men become Christians. Many women said that they believe this is true. Asked why, Joanna said that women need other women to talk to and relate to, while Barbara felt that women are gentler and more open and willing to give themselves to "a person as loving and dear as Jesus who loves us no matter what we look like, warts and all."

Jenny made a similar point, observing that "men seem happier with the caveman image and are encouraged in their 'maleness,' so 'love' has only a small part in their makeup." Gillian thinks "men are encouraged by society to be self-sufficient, in control, not owing anything to anyone. It is not easy for a man to admit to dependence on *anyone*." Wilma's perspective is slightly different. "Men like to think they are macho and in control of their lives. Therefore they don't see the need in their lives for Jesus." One husband, Tim, who completed a questionnaire, suspects it has to do with "arrogance—I don't think I could accept that degree of humility that worship demands."

Others, like Irene, focused on another male tendency. She says, "I think that, generally, men look for scientific reasoning more than women: 'I must see it to believe it.'" Sue endorses this as she explained why she thinks her husband does not believe. "I think it's because you cannot see Jesus in person. If you cannot see it, it cannot be." This, of course, was precisely the reason that Thomas, one of Jesus' disciples, gave for not believing that the resurrection had happened. "Unless I see the nail marks in his hands and put my finger where the nails were, and put my hand into his side, I will not believe it," he said (Jn 20:25).

Even though they cannot see the risen Jesus today, husbands who find it difficult or nearly impossible to believe in Jesus can be faced with other powerful evidence that Christianity is real. If a man has shared his life with his wife for some years, he should know her fairly well. If she then becomes a Christian, and besides starting to attend church also begins to change for the better as a person, her husband may note the significance in the timing.

In these circumstances a husband may begin to work this through. He may puzzle over what he has noticed is happening to his wife. This may directly challenge his indifference, agnosticism, or atheism. He may not like the implications of what he senses is happening and may still write Christianity off for himself. However, he is being challenged by something that seems to be affecting his wife beneficially.

FEAR

A man who detects changes in his wife may feel genuine fear if he does not see Christianity as compatible with his own image. Before she and her husband separated, Stephanie was sure that he understood the power and reality of the Christian faith. She was twenty-nine and pregnant when she became a Christian, and she believes her husband saw God's power to change lives. "That's why he's afraid," she discloses. "He's fascinated and longing for it himself, but he feels unworthy."

Carly's husband may be afraid of committing his life to Christ, despite seeing changes in his wife. She became a Christian shortly after getting married. Commenting on why she thinks her husband does not yet believe, she says, "He believes in the Lord but appears afraid to take that final step in accepting Christ. It seems too easy; there must be a catch somewhere!"

Asked the same question about her husband, Sandra says, "He is a scientist and engineer and everything has to be black or white. If anyone at church acts in any kind of un-Christian way, he immediately states that this is why he doesn't want to have anything to do with church. In my view, he is afraid of commitment."

RETICENCE

Many men whose wives are committed Christians are uncertain what to make of Jesus Christ. David's view is that he is "not concerned if he did or did not exist; it does not affect the way I think." Neil says, "I do believe in Jesus Christ, but it seems that people always expect you to show how much and prove the extent." Clearly, he is reluctant to do this.

This raises an important point. Derek and Lilian Cook, evangelists whose ministry includes helping Christian wives with husbands who do not yet believe, teach that men do not want to be hypocrites.[11] A man may believe in Jesus Christ to some extent, but he knows from experience that if he attends church he will end up having to sing hymns and say prayers which include words and sentiments that he is not yet ready to express. To stand there while others around him are fully involved is embarrassing; to participate when he cannot do so with integrity is hypocritical. Even though he could be interested in exploring Christianity further, he is reluctant to go to church because he does not want to look foolish or be untrue to himself.

BEREAVEMENT

It is a fallacy to imagine that people are bereaved only when a close relative or friend dies. People go through the bereavement process at any time in life when they experience severe loss. Maybe they lose something valuable, or it is stolen; their job and career may be snatched from them by a layoff or early retirement. For some, it will be traumatic if a child leaves home to go to college or to get married. Others will have to cope with the pain of marital separation and divorce.

A non-Christian husband may go through similar anguish if he feels that his spouse is no longer "his." Imagine two people who marry and devote themselves to each other. They enjoy one another's company, spend a lot of time together, and share some similar interests. The wife becomes a Christian and, having discovered both Jesus and his church, wants to grow and develop in the faith. The effect on her partner can be considerable. Whereas before, she focused much of her attention on him, she now has an outside interest that seems highly important to her. It could have been a hobby that consumed her and that would have been bad enough. Within Christianity, however, she has found a person called Jesus with whom she claims to have a love relationship. To the partner left on the sidelines, this can be devastating news. He perceives that their marriage has been attacked by an outside agency claiming his wife's heart.

He senses the loss of the earlier relationship with his spouse very deeply, even though the two of them still share the same home and bed. He feels that the exclusive, mutual love they had earlier is no longer there.

ANGER

Some husbands get angry following the conversion of their wives to Christianity. It is not so much that they object to their wives finding faith in Christ or going to church on Sundays; it is more the extras that begin to intrude into the previously settled life of the family.

Husbands often feel it is acceptable if their wives go out to occasional evening meetings during the week. Some wives may want to get involved in events on Saturday. What irritated one man greatly was his own home being used for Christian meetings when his wife and children were believers and he was not. Joyce Huggett knew him and says that when his house was used frequently for meetings, ultimately "he was forced to protest. The sanctuary he needed when he returned home after a draining day at work was being invaded."[12] Both Joyce and I have sympathy for him, believing this intrusion to be inappropriate and insensitive.

In situations like this a change of strategy may remove the husband's anger. Joyce and the man's wife discussed the problem and...

realized what he needed was not to be evangelized but to be loved. He needed to have his worth as a faithful husband and good father affirmed and appreciated. This worked wonders. I am not saying he too became a Christian—he didn't. What did happen was that harmony was restored to the home. He later confided in his wife: "You"re the closest friend I have and I value that highly."[13]

Unbelieving partners have as much right to express righteous anger as do committed Christians, and if they sense they are being treated unfairly it is not unreasonable for them to say so. When this happens, it helps enormously if the Christian partner has the maturity and objectivity to be able to view things from the other person's point of view.

David is another husband who feels angry. "She sometimes 'preaches' to me what is right or wrong, which annoys me," he says. Donna reports that her husband "sees her faith as an illness and is angry and embarrassed." She perceives that they are traveling spiritually in opposite directions.

Jill's husband was angry for a different reason. After she became a Christian, "he expected me to lie or falsify things. He had to realize that I will not do it," she says. In this situation, Jill had to tolerate his displeasure because she was not prepared to compromise her newfound faith.

BEING USED

David Bennett is an honest man. In order to help Christian wives understand the circumstances of their (as yet) non-Christian husbands, he wrote *An Open Letter from a Church Widower*. In it he refers to the lists he makes of jobs to do when the family is at church. He needs, however, to help them get there first before he can get started. He refers to himself as "the back-up team" for the Christians in the family. He is the transportation department, as well as the chef who prepares and cooks Sunday lunch. He helps people in the church with practical jobs, undertakes babysitting, designs and makes the set for the church play, and before the show begins, even gets "his statutory dose of the church bore!"[14]

While David Bennett seems to enjoy what he does, other husbands may not. They may feel it is an imposition that the church seems to take for granted their voluntary help. In such circumstances it would not be unusual for some husbands to feel used and trapped. This is unhelpful at best and could provoke a rift and growing resentment toward both the family and the church.

In the case of Madeleine's husband, he is angry because he feels she is being taken advantage of by the church. "He knows I worship and am deeply committed, and therefore I have a 'secret' over which he has no control. He does not approve of money or time spent on Christian friends. His expression is that I am being 'used.'" As he sees it, his wife's circumstances are a good reason why he should stay clear of church himself.

RESENTMENT

The unbelieving partners of Christians sometimes struggle with resentment if they detect that the Christian spouses have found something that has clearly made a life-changing impression. Dave had been a fringe Christian for a year or two when he married Shirley. As his Christian life developed and God became more important to him, he found that Shirley became resentful on two grounds. "She doesn't mind my taking our two small boys to church on Sundays," he says, but she regards his putting God higher on his list of priorities in life as "an invasion of our family life." His perception is that "she resents the fact that I'm so happy and clearly have something she doesn't."[15]

You might think that this feeling in itself would be enough to encourage someone to explore Christianity personally. Sadly, this does not always happen. An unbelieving partner, despite being unhappy, may choose to stay in that emotional state for a long period. It will almost certainly cause problems in the home because resentment is a breeding ground for negative attitudes. Dave says of his situation, "It causes great strain between us. At times our marriage has been near break-up."[16]

Gillian's life has also been difficult since she came to Christ. "My husband found it impossible to understand why I suddenly needed God and the company of other Christians. He states very strongly that 'he doesn't believe in God.' He doesn't want me to speak of my Christian life to him. Although he appears to tolerate my going to church and teaching in Sunday school, he resents it very much.... He resents friends I have there and thinks my time and loyalty should be devoted to him."

This is also Daniel's view of his wife's involvement in her church. "What she does (arranging flowers in church and attending meetings) takes up too much time," he says. Abigail says that her husband sees things similarly. "Occasionally he becomes resentful of the time I give to the Lord in both church activities and study of his Word."

It is deeply regrettable when both marriage and family life are hampered for a long time by continuing resentment in at least one of the partners. Until they are ready to release it, however, there is little anyone can do—except, of course, to pray.

Hazel says that this is what she does every day. She can testify now that life at home is considerably easier. "In the beginning he resented the change in me and thought I would grow out of it. We have lived through all the usual problems and difficulties, but now he completely accepts that I am a Christian and want to do some things he does not want to do. It is no problem." Hazel's story will encourage other wives to keep praying too.

HOSTILITY

There are occasions when a husband or wife never seems able to accept that his or her partner's life is committed to Jesus Christ. Anne became a Christian when she attended the church for her school-age daughter's baptism. Her husband Tom went too, but remained unmoved.

Tom was, and still is, very hostile to Anne's faith and any church-related activity. He has agreed to Anne attending Sunday morning services and the weekly house group [small group] meeting, but Anne feels unable to participate in other activities because Tom is home during the day. Phone calls to and from friends can bring forth angry criticism. Christian friends do not feel free to come by, and overtly Christian books are kept out of the way, without being actually hidden. Anne gave up a good, paid, part-time job in the church in the face of Tom's opposition, and stayed at home for six sad and frustrating months out of respect for his feelings.[17]

Research has shown that, following the conversion of their wives to Christianity, 12 percent of husbands become increasingly hostile as time goes on. This hostility is expressed verbally and sometimes physically. Derek and Lilian Cook, who have published their research findings, say that such hostility "may be linked to deep problems in the man's life. Husbands might be bitter already because of ill health or unemployment."[18]

Jill says that her husband admits he is "a very moody and hot-tempered person. I share with him what Jesus has done for me by dying on the cross. He tells me that he doesn't want to know; he's all right. He tells me that I am evil and need to go to church, which I admit because I am not perfect and need my Lord's help every day. I do hold back because it only causes trouble and he gets so worked up."

When in a situation like Anne's or Jill's, the only way to hold your marriage together and attempt to be loyal to Jesus is to pray a lot, encourage Christian friends to pray for you, and tread tactfully and sensitively at home.

THE SUPPORTIVE SPOUSE

Not every marriage hits hard times when one partner starts to follow Jesus. Five years after she married Doug, Angela became a Christian. She admits she longed to tell her husband how she felt about Jesus, but she didn't know how to.

"I sometimes seemed almost brusque, trying to play it down when all the time I was dying to let it all out," she says. One of the things Angela appreciates is that Doug has not objected to bringing up the children in a Christian way. He has even encouraged her to get involved in church activities.[19]

Whether we understand it or not, some people like the ethics of Christianity and try to live good, respectable lives, without ever feeling the motivation or need to become personal followers of Jesus. They appreciate what the church stands for and seeks to do, and are happy to encourage others to be part of it and loyal Christians. However, they do not see why they should move in this direction themselves, and so stay on the sidelines.

Carly puts her husband in this category. "My husband is very supportive toward me and my children's work in the church. I believe he admires my faith and that of other church members, but can't relate to them." Pauline's husband thinks Christianity "is a fairy tale! He was brought up in the Catholic faith and said he had enough of religion when he was a child. But he always encourages me to attend church."

INTEREST

Some husbands, however, find something begins to interest them in their wives' newfound faith, although not necessarily immediately after their wives' conversions. In their research, Derek and Lilian Cook discovered that approximately 15 percent of husbands surveyed are "beginning to change. Previously neutral or busy, now they are starting to ask questions and attend events. They are interested!"[20] Mavis believes her husband is in this position. There are no problems between them caused by her faith "because my husband is very supportive, interested, and searching."

As we saw from Engel's Scale in chapter three, few people become Christians without first going through a period of searching. All of us need time to ask questions, reflect on what we discover, and decide our response to the claims of Christ. When a husband starts to display some interest in the teaching of the Bible and church, it shows that something may have started to happen inside him. This can only be encouraging, but be warned: until he makes his own commitment to Christ and tells you about it, he needs to be given space, time, and a lot of gentle, sensitive prayer support.

Many writers tell stories of unconverted husbands or wives who eventually came to believe in Jesus for themselves. It is the dream of most Christian wives that their husbands will be next! Having reviewed some of the ways a husband responds when his wife starts believing in Christ, we will now see what contribution a wife in this situation can take to encourage him on his way.

CHAPTER FIVE

How Can You Help Your Husband?

Sadness is a common emotion among wives answering the question, "How do you feel about the fact that your husband is not a Christian?" Christian wives whose husbands do not share their faith tend to be unhappy and discontented with things as they are. One wife says, "I feel very sad my husband is not a Christian." Another Christian wife agrees: "I am sad, very sad, because he would feel he was a better person, more confident in himself, and mostly, would have a father in a way he has never known one."

The Bible teaches that God has a missionary nature. As a God of compassion as well as justice, he wants the people he has created on earth to understand how deeply he loves them and to respond to his love by loving him freely in return. God loves your husband just as much as he loves you, even if your husband shows no signs of positive response.

In this chapter we will see how God can break into your husband's life in the same way as he has into yours. From the beginning, however, we must understand that there is no guarantee that, if we take certain steps, God will work in some kind of programmed way.

When talking to Nicodemus, Jesus emphasized the need for this Jewish Pharisee to be born-again by "water and the Spirit" (Jn 3:5). Jesus taught that this only happens when the Holy Spirit works in a person's life; he contrasted it to being born physically as a baby. Yet his activity and influence cannot be controlled humanly any more than people can affect the direction and strength of the wind. "The wind blows wherever it pleases," Jesus said. "You hear its sound, but you cannot tell where it comes from or where it is going. So it is with everyone born of the Spirit" (Jn 3:8).

I can give you no assurance that your husband will believe in Jesus if you use the stratagems explained in this chapter. However, they are unlikely to have any harmful effect, so you have little to lose. What is certain is that God, who knows your heart and motives, has the capacity to bless you for praying and working toward the goal of your husband's conversion whether or not it happens during your lifetime.

In chapter four we noted some differences between men and women. We now return to this subject in more depth, as we begin to see how you can best help your husband discover God.

TRY TO UNDERSTAND MEN

No one pretends it is easy to understand the opposite sex. Also, we must remember that some of us from both sexes have been brought up on a pack of lies and deceit which have colored our views of the roles of both men and women. Many of these are cultural, but they often affect Bible-believing Christians just as much as anyone else, until they see them for what they are.

Christine Noble has listed a number of these false barriers which, she argues, should be dismantled because they are untrue. First of all, five untruths about women:

- Women were made to be married.
- A woman's place is in the home.
- Babies and children are the woman's responsibility.
- Women are best equipped for housework and cooking.
- Women are not logical.

Equally, she says, there are lies that circulate about men:
- Men must work to support their families.
- Men are not interested in babies.
- Carpentry, decorating, car maintenance, and finances are male responsibilities.
- Men are not emotional or intuitive.
- Men and boys shouldn't cry.
- Men should always take the lead.[1]

While these comments may describe what seems to be the cultural norm in Western society, they are not consistent with the truth of God as revealed in the Bible. None of these statements about either women or men is to be found there, and yet many Christians live as if they are.

If you want God to use you to help your husband find Christ, you need to understand more about men. Derek and Lilian Cook teach some sociological facts as part of their *Husbands and the Kingdom* seminars.[2]

Men are not good at words. Research shows that while women use both sides of their brain to form words, men use only the left side. This gives them a disadvantage when it comes to speaking.

Men are competitive. Because they are competitive, men are less likely to have close male friends than women are to have close female friends. Other men may be viewed with a degree of suspicion. It follows, therefore, that if his wife becomes a Christian, a man may feel that she has beaten him to the finish line in the race to find out what eternal life is all about.

Men do not want to be hypocrites. Some men will not find it easy to discover the truth about Christianity if they first have to go to worship services where they are obliged to take an active part. A man will feel unable to say prayers, or sing hymns or songs with expressions of praise or gratitude that he does not share.

Men are easily embarrassed. Unfamiliar territory makes men nervous, especially if they find they are expected to do things in a certain way or at a given time. Church is a place where they can become easily embarrassed because they will not know what to do. This does not mean that some men will not do things *for* the church; they view this quite differently from going *to* church. It is much more safe and predictable because *they* set the parameters and remain in some degree of control.

Men are always looking for strength. Christianity is commonly perceived as being for weak people. It is considered a crutch for those who are vulnerable to life's knocks. In trusting in Jesus Christ, they tap into a source of outside strength to compensate for their own internal weaknesses. Men do not like to admit weakness, and therefore tend to have a natural dislike of Christianity, until the real truth about it dawns on them. Men would have a healthier respect for Christianity if they were aware how demanding it is to be a loyal disciple of Jesus Christ. If they could see the manliness of Jesus in perspective, and grasp the spiritual, intellectual, and physical demands of following him, many men would immediately gain a respect both for the Christian faith and Christian people.

Derek and Lilian Cook's insights help us see where many men stand. They also identify five stages a man goes through in his life, although these may be less applicable in times of economic recession and high unemployment.

The "upward and onward" years (20-30). These are tense years when a man establishes himself at work and maybe as a husband and parent too. In choosing his wife he selects a woman who will be a mother (to care for him), a "movie star" (to add glamour to his life), and a Joan-of-Arc (to fight battles with him).

The "consolidation" years (35-45). At this time in a man's life he builds on the accomplishments of his past.

Mid-life crisis (40... 45... 50). This is a period when a man may have crazy ideas. He sometimes feels he needs to escape from the pressures of life. At this time he stops saying, "if I die..." and says "when I die...." Often he will conclude that he has not yet done anything worthwhile in his life. He also knows by now that he will never achieve most of his ideals. For some men this stage may begin in their late thirties.

The years of peace (50-65). If a man has a purposeful life, he can relax a little and begin to enjoy what he now knows are only a limited number of active years ahead. However, if his life is not purposeful, he may live with growing frustration because he has less opportunity to influence events.

The retirement years (65 and over). This period is something new (unless he has been unemployed earlier in life). Some men struggle to adjust to life in retirement and many seemingly healthy men die in the first two years after they cease work. He will need new goals and may well turn his hobbies into a job because he feels that without a job he does not exist.

PRACTICAL IDEAS

If your desire is to see God work in your husband's life, there are things you can do in close cooperation with God to help make him more open to Jesus Christ and your personal faith. In chapter three we identified your prayers as a major force that God will use. What follows are practical, yet spiritual, actions that you can take alongside your constant praying.

Put him first. It is very easy to take your partner for granted once you are married to him. Life can go on day after day without you thinking about your relationship. But if your wedding ceremony was in church, you probably made profound promises to put your partner first, even before yourself. The Anglican *Alternative Service Book* includes the following words in the wedding service:

> I, (name), take you, (name),
> to be my wife (husband),
> to have and to hold
> from this day forward;
> for better, for worse,
> for richer, for poorer,
> in sickness and in health,
> to love and to cherish,
> till death us do part,
> according to God's holy law;
> and this is my solemn vow.[3]

Being self-centered is natural for human beings. To put anyone else first takes resolve and effort, but this is what marriage is all about.

Here is a major difference between God and ourselves. His love for human beings is so rich that he gave his Son completely and unselfishly for us. When a Christian spouse lets God's love enter and flow through him or her, an unbelieving partner should notice something different. Joyce Huggett suggests that when you wake up in the morning you should ask, "How can I make my partner happy today?" When the Christian in the relationship acts on this, she says, "very often, the partner begins to sit up, to take notice, to ask significant questions about God and his way of doing things."[4] To put this into practice is costly, but it can be very effective.

Enjoy sex together. Before we marry and become part of a relationship where we can have enjoyable and fulfilling sexual experiences, we may wonder how sex can ever get stale. Yet for some couples it can and it does. Intercourse becomes routine, mechanical, or virtually nonexistent, and the whole concept of fun-filled sex seems a million miles away.

Even if the sexual side of your marriage is enjoyable and satisfying, it could be that with more thought and preparation it could have a rejuvenating effect on your whole relationship!

The reason I encourage this is because the Bible shows that sexual intimacy, within the stable and committed environment of marriage, is part of God's plan. Of course, sexual intercourse is the Creator's way of ensuring the continuation of the human race, yet there is no reference to procreation in many of the Biblical passages that allude to the sexual relationship that can be enjoyed within a marriage. (See Genesis 2:24, Proverbs 5:18-19, Song of Songs 4.)

God knew, when he made people, that they would need the intimacy and encouragement which lovemaking gives. When it is part of marriage, sexual intercourse provides a heartfelt and joyous way of expressing love and commitment to our partner while, at the same time, bringing enrichment to both. The more that a Christian wife genuinely can enjoy the sexual side of the relationship with her husband, the more he will feel loved, valued, and appreciated. This in turn may encourage him to reflect more on the many positive qualities of his wife, including, maybe, her faith in God.

Have fun together. In the same way that sex can become dull, so can life in general. When your honeymoon feels like ancient history and your current work and home life is fairly predictable, the fun of your courtship days may seem very distant. Maybe you view yourself now as a stable and mature adult compared with the carefree and immature person you were when you were courting. Perhaps you are more serious about your faith now and feel that you should not be frivolous as a Christian.

Counselor Zelda West-Meads is quoted in a magazine article as saying that whether a couple has fun together is a major factor that affects the success or failure of their relationship. "Fun is very important. One thing that you see when marriages run into trouble is that couples are not talking together, spending enough time together, doing things that attracted them to each other in the first place. It's the sort of thing that couples can easily let slip, particularly if they are both in full-time jobs or have young children."[5]

Recognizing that having fun together is easier said than done, Joyce Huggett emphasizes the need for us to "carve out quality time to be with our partner." It is essential, she says, for us "to assure them that we still value their friendship."[6] When life is routine and we have jobs to do and meetings to attend, cultivating the friendship with your spouse may be the last thing on your mind. If we neglect this and do not make time to be together regularly where we can enjoy each other's company, we not only put the relationship at risk, but also make it harder for an unbelieving spouse to come to faith. A husband who is not yet committed to Christ is likely to be more open to his wife's faith if their relationship is fresh and vibrant.

Naomi Starkey suggests five fun things that you can do:

- Gaze into each other's eyes. With small children around, it's easy to forget to look at your partner!
- Have a kiss-and-cuddle session on the sofa.
- Take a picnic breakfast out somewhere.
- Dig out your old love letters and read them aloud.
- Try a new activity, just for a laugh: skiing; hang gliding; trampolining.[7]

Stay attractive. You only have to look at adolescents to see how instinctive it is for them to dress to look appealing to the opposite sex. Once a girl has found and caught her man, and the years have rolled on, it is easy, and in some ways not unnatural, for her to feel that dressing to attract his attention is now totally unnecessary. She is his and he is hers anyway. Men can also begin to dress in a slovenly manner once they feel they have no one they need to impress.

It can only help your continuing relationship with your husband if you avoid becoming dull, dour, or dreary.[8] He may not say much, but is bound to notice if you let yourself go. He undoubtedly wants you to remain as attractive as you were when you first met and fell for each other. If he feels genuinely proud to be with you in public, it can only help your relationship with him in private.

Get your church involved. God expects you, as a Christian, to be involved actively in the life of a church near where you live. He has never intended that you (or anyone else) should be a disciple of Jesus in isolation. If, then, you are part of a local church fellowship, you do not have to carry the weight of any of your domestic problems on your own.

Paul encourages the Christians in Rome to support one another within their church. "We who are strong ought to bear with the failings of the weak and not to please ourselves. Each of us should please his neighbor for his good, to build him up" (Rom 15:1-2). In the light of this, we have a responsibility to share our lives with others in our churches, so that God can use us all to provide mutual support for one another.

Here are four ways in which your church may be able to help support you as a wife whose husband does not share her faith.

Try corporate prayer. It is probable that there are other Christian wives in your church whose home situation is similar to yours. Encourage other wives to join you in special times of prayer. Pray, of course, for all the husbands, but also use the time to discover, both by discreet conversation and by listening to God, which husband appears to be the most responsive to the gospel at the present time. You can then particularly focus your prayers that he will see his need of Jesus. When he has made his own response to Jesus, however short or long a time this takes, pray that he can be the human means by which the other men meet Jesus too.[9]

When it comes to your own husband, how you pray and what you pray for is important. As far as you can, focus your prayers on what you sense are the reasons why he has not yet become a believer in Christ. During my research I learned that some wives are uncertain why their husbands have not become Christians. You and those who pray with and for you can ask the Holy Spirit to help you understand. Even though your husband has not revealed his reasons for holding back, the Holy Spirit knows and can give you divine guidance and insight.

Some wives, like Gillian, have heard their husbands say many times why they have not accepted Christ. Her husband "thinks religion is for those who can't cope. He says he is in control of his life and doesn't need to worry about finding the meaning of life." Wilma thinks her husband's reluctance to follow Jesus is "because he is afraid of what his friends will say and of the changes it will make to his life." Carly's husband is an intellectual and he needs to have, she says, "evidence and proof for everything."

No one becomes a Christian without first receiving spiritual revelation from God. God knows in detail the inner workings of people's minds and hearts, and he gives precisely the understanding and illumination each one needs. It is when we pray that God so often gives these. Prayer is vital if husbands are to find Christ.

Churches can be more helpful. The way many churches function almost makes it harder, not easier, for men to become

Christians and then be integrated successfully into a local church. There are three factors we need to understand that are common in churches, in order that we can consider possible changes in policy or emphasis. Once we have seen the need, we can ask for God's help before deciding how best to broach this with the leadership.

A. Churches tend to encourage passivity. Many parents know that boys are inclined to be more aggressive than girls. As this tendency carries on into adult life, it means, as Gavin Wakefield reminds us, "that men are not so good at being passive and receptive, which is what most of our churches expect of the congregation."[10] If men had more opportunities to serve God within the ministry of the church, it would help them feel more comfortable there. In order to feel integrated, men need a role to fulfill.

B. Churches tend to frown on self-reliance and independence. In many cultures, including those in the West, girls are often brought up to take their place in society as those who nurture, submit, and are loyal. Boys are encouraged to become self-reliant and independent. In due course, the responsibility of providing for wife and family will rest firmly on their shoulders. To cope with this successfully, they may have to be creative, innovative, and take some risks. "In most churches obedience and responsibility are viewed positively, self-reliance and independence negatively. Given that, it's not surprising that more women than men respond positively to what they see and hear in church."[11]

The irony is that while self-reliance and independence are tendencies that make a man depend on himself and his own judgement, God is looking for people who will be creative, innovative, and take risks. The major difference lies in whom they trust. In Hebrews 11 we read of some of the great men and women of faith. We are encouraged to emulate the way they listened to God, had simple trust in him, and were willing to take risks. Today's churches are in desperate need of dedicated Christian men who will follow example.

C. Churches tend to cater best to women. The way some churches are organized makes it harder for men to get involved. Gavin Wakefield highlights some common factors:

- **Strange rituals.** "Men feel awkward about doing the wrong thing. Whether it's the requirements of a prayer book, or the unwritten requirements of a liturgy, we don't want to let ourselves down by getting it wrong."

- **Intimacy.** "In our culture men get more embarrassed about sharing personal details such as feelings, worries, problems..." so Christian education classes and small groups often make the female/male imbalance seem even worse.

- **Children's work.** "This is often a very visible part of the church's ministry, and reinforces the idea that church is for women and children, especially if the leaders of such work are mainly women."

- **Ministers.** "Ministers in the past often called when only the woman was at home anyway. Even when they do meet the man, there is often quite a gulf because of such different working experiences."

- **Time.** "What are the men in your church doing? Apart from possibly being husbands, fathers, and out at work, are they also... group leaders, musicians, and elders, all at once? Friendship with other men is a very important step in most conversions, but it takes time. Do the Christian men you know have the time—and the church's backing—to develop such friendships?"[12]

Churches can initiate appropriate, good-quality events. Naturally, you want your husband to hear the Good News of Jesus from time to time, but you need to be careful how you arrange this. If your church's family service is full of noisy children, it may be best not to encourage your husband to go with you; he may find it distracting and tiresome.[13]

If your church organizes a carol service, Christmas party, barn dance, or starts to present "seeker-friendly services" based on the style of Chicago's highly successful Willow Creek Community Church, it may be very appropriate to invite your husband to go with you. You can encourage your friends to pray with and for you as you ask him.

Some statistics that emerged from my survey of Christian wives whose husbands do not share their faith concern the extent to which the men come to services or other events at the wife's church. From 131 completed questionnaires, 9 percent of wives said that their husbands attend church regularly, 55 percent said they come occasionally, while 36 percent said they never come. If this is a representative sample, it suggests that only a little more than a third of the husbands are so strongly opposed to Christianity and the church that they will have no contact with it at all. The opportunity seems to exist, therefore, for churches to create imaginative events which many of these husbands might attend, if invited in the right way.

Churches should eliminate what may be unhelpful. It may sound bizarre, but while many churches are supposedly committed to reaching out to people with the Good News of Jesus, they are simultaneously making it harder for some people to believe in him. Some of the answers given in my research show this.

I asked wives to describe occasions when they felt herchurch or fellow Christians seemed more of a hindrance than a help to their husbands becoming Christians. I received some worrisome replies. Julie says that she feels very uneasy when Christians talk critically about other Christians in front of their husband, and when they arrogantly speak as if they have got it right and he is merely a poor unbeliever. Jennifer is unhappy when Christians start to force their beliefs and opinions on her husband. Barbara refers to Christian friends who come across as "too holy" when they "talk of visions and get very fervent." She says that her husband just switches off.

Wilma tells of one occasion when her husband went to church with her and everyone was very nice to him. Next day, when he was in his working clothes and went to speak to one of the same people, they didn't seem to recognize him. It turned him off to church. Deborah's response is more general. "When people try to force Christianity on him, it stirs up his animosity. If they are gentle in their approach and respect him, he'll listen."

Gillian's husband was put off by the church service. "He did once come to a service and found the very charismatic style, and especially the words of the choruses, a total turn-off. Some people, too, give the impression he's a soul to be saved, not an individual to befriend and get to know. He is a desperately lonely and isolated person, but he wants people, not just Jesus."

I do not know what will happen next in your husband's life, but perhaps the miracle for which you yearn will take place. It is important that you realize that this is not *your* responsibility. It is between God and your husband, and all your praying and hard work cannot make him a follower of Jesus, although God can use these things as contributing factors. One wife who feels she is not "nearly good enough a witness" at home, has nevertheless understood. "I know Alan's salvation is not dependent on my witness, but feel it would help," she says. She is right, of course. It is when our witness and actions dovetail into God's plans and purposes that he is able to work powerfully on earth.

PART THREE

All About
Your Children

CHAPTER SIX

What Effects Do Children Feel?

In many respects it seems grossly unfair that children should be caught up in the problems of their parents' relationship. It is inevitable that they will be, because any tensions in a home cannot be avoided by those who live there. Sadly, this is just as much true when the problems concern the parents' faith, or lack of it, as with any other issue.

In this chapter and the next we will explore the effects that serious faith-related problems in a marriage can have on the children. If you do not have children living at home, you may choose to turn straight to chapter eight.

AREAS OF CONFLICT

What to do on Sundays. Sunday has been special for Christians ever since Jesus Christ rose from the dead on the first day of the week. The New Testament shows that whereas the Jews kept Saturday as their Sabbath, Christians restructured their week after Jesus' resurrection. They believed that every Sunday should be a day of celebration that the Head of the Church is alive forever and Lord of all.

Few would want to deny Christians the freedom to worship together on Sundays, but in many countries, Sunday has become just another day for business with leisure and recreational facilities open and widely available. All this makes the situation harder where there is a division over faith. The issue of which activity should take precedence causes turmoil in some families.

Janice says that her husband encourages her "in my 'church life,' as he calls it, but doesn't encourage my son to attend his church group as much as I do, which can cause a bit of friction." Donna's situation is more traumatic. Her husband sees her faith as an illness. "We have experienced frightening family uproars before departing for church," she says. "If you're going to brainwash them with that rubbish," he threatens, "I'll brainwash them with the opposite" (by which he means black magic).

Jasmine finds difficulty with her children's comments. Her husband "won't come to church to see the children in Sunday school concerts, or join in family services. The children see other dads with their children and want to know why he's not there." Sue's frustration is her inability to influence her children as fully as she would like. She "would like the children to go to church every week, but sometimes they need a gentle push. My husband does not allow this, so they only go when they really want to—which is not very often."

Sarah can see that the problems her husband has with Christianity will get worse soon. "The two older children accompany me to church at present, while he stays at home to look after the youngest. The older two see this as the reason he doesn't come to church. He says he doesn't know how he will confront the issue when the youngest is old enough to come with us, and he really doesn't see how he will be able to make them come when he objects to coming himself. In short, church attendance is the problem rather than Christianity itself."

The way all this affects children is not easy to quantify. It is disruptive if children have an erratic program on Sundays, so that sometimes they attend church and sometimes they do not. The lack of continuity means that in churches where they are taught the Bible sequentially, they cannot grasp the complete flow of a passage or story. It is also disruptive to their relationships when they are unable to say for certain whether or not they will be there next week. This certainly puts them at a disadvantage compared to other children, and makes them feel different from those whose parents seem to have more settled lives.

Christian teaching. The main responsibility for preparing children for life in the big wide world lies with the parents although, in practice, parents and schools cooperate to prepare children to live and work as adults.

Complications arise when there are fundamental disagreements within a home as to what and how parents should teach their children. While a couple should have resolved many of these problems before they married, or at least before they chose to have children, some are unavoidable because circumstances change.

One change is a wife becoming a Christian after her marriage, while her husband remains an unbeliever. It may mean that the husband and wife, as parents, have differing views about how much Christian teaching they can pass on to the children.

Karen and Sonya have this problem. Karen's husband "is often scornful and ridicules me for my faith in front of anyone. He does not feel a need to obey God's laws. Therefore we have conflict in bringing up our children and in our outlook on life." Sonya says, "My husband's points of view about raising the children are obviously a lot different from mine, but I encourage and teach my daughter and son when we are on our own. I often find a lot of things that he says to them very upsetting."

When one parent believes it is his or her God-given duty to teach the children about God, the other may become skeptical, fearing that the children will be indoctrinated. My research suggests that many unbelieving husbands have a serious fear that someone will indoctrinate their children—either their mother at home, or others at church.

Jasminder's husband thinks this way. Jasminder used to be a Hindu, but has now become a Christian, and wants to help her children get to know the Lord. Her husband, who is not a Hindu, does not approve of this and says that no one must take their choice away from them. Jasminder, reflecting on his response, says, "'Choice' seems to be the operative word here. I see this as an excuse."

Sandra does not find life at home very easy either. "My husband tells the children that religion is 'a load of old rubbish,' and while I wanted them to attend Sunday school, he said they needn't if they don't want to. Guess who won." Hilary's situation was similar, but has now improved. "My husband did not want the children to be brainwashed. He did not allow me to pray at the dinner table. But now I've been a Christian for such a long time he never discourages the children and he supports me on moral issues too."

Vicki says that this issue is at the heart of the problems between herself and her husband. "He is very worried about me taking our son to church because he thinks it is 'brainwashing.' At the moment it's not too bad because our son is nursery-age (and I help to run the nursery), but when he is three he will be eligible to start Sunday school. My husband has already said that he doesn't want our son to go, which will put me in a very difficult position. At the moment I keep taking Robert to the nursery and am just dreading his third birthday."

If children have to cope with a contentious atmosphere at home, they will always find this hard to bear. When they love both parents equally, they find themselves caught between the two. One parent believes the Bible is the inspired word of God; the other may see it simply as a book of religious writings. One believes in the existence of a loving and caring God;

the other may not accept that he is there at all. One believes that our lives on earth can be greatly enhanced if we believe in Jesus Christ and seek to follow him; the other thinks this is merely fanciful. One believes that prayer is meaningful communication with the living God; the other thinks that anyone who prays is seriously deluded. In between are the children, who find this difference of views between two people whom they love both alarming and baffling.

Philippa says, "My husband sometimes talks about his unbelief, causing some confusion for our twelve-year-old daughter." The result can be that the children may not know what to accept and believe. However, Isobel felt encouraged by what happened after her sons attended church for many years. "One day I overheard a discussion in my eldest son's bedroom with his friends. They had a mixed-up concept of religion. My son was able to put them straight. He *had* been listening all these years at Bible Club!"

Moral standards. Further difficulties arise in families when parents with different religious beliefs, or none at all, encourage their children to adopt varying moral standards that will affect their decisions as adolescents and adults. Whether we like it or not, there is sometimes a huge difference between moral standards based on God's truth, and others that are acceptable to those with no living faith.

The reason for this is simple. God has called those who believe in him to model their lives on his purity and righteousness. "Be holy, because I am holy," he told the Jewish people (Lev 11:44). He gave the Jews a set of commandments to keep which would help them to relate responsibly and honorably, both to him and to their neighbors (Ex 20:1-17). Because God is wholly moral, he taught his people that they needed to live upright lives to please him. The teachings of Jesus and the New Testament writers confirms this. God expects disciples of Jesus to follow him, not only in a general sense, but in terms of their lifestyle and moral code too.

Whereas Christians have fixed ethical standards set down for them in the Bible by which they can aim to live, those without a living faith in God may have nothing at all. They may well rely on "situation ethics" where, with few if any fixed standards as to what is morally right, the best and most fair decision that can be made at that time is agreed.

The difference between the two approaches can be enormous. The Bible forbids sex outside marriage, and teaches that God devised intercourse to enrich marriage relationships of love and commitment. However, to those who have no particular regard for God and his truth and who take a humanistic view, intercourse outside marriage may seem perfectly normal, acceptable, and quite harmless. The same is true of trial marriages and couples living together.

When a child grows up in a family where the parents disagree on acceptable standards of behavior and language, they are highly likely to become puzzled until they are mature enough to reach their own conclusions. In the meantime they find themselves embroiled in debates about the acceptability of certain books and videos, and about standards of behavior and speech. Unless their parents can find ways to agree, the children may become seriously confused because they are in close touch with very different role models.

Diana's home is like this. "We sometimes give differing opinions on issues that crop up, and this can make it difficult for our children to know what to accept. My husband has spoken to our son about evolution and moral issues like sex before marriage, couples living together, small lies, and cheating. I also give my views and pray that my husband will have his eyes opened to the truth and that the children will be protected against all that is evil."

Maggie's situation is similar. "I always try to live by my Christian principles, but we disagree sometimes on what the girls watch on television, what they read, and about boyfriends. I have often had to back down in an argument as I don't feel it is right for the girls to see us with conflicting opinions, as they get confused." Linda says, "There are things which I probably wouldn't allow or don't like, but if I complain I'm told that this is how things are in the world and I can't protect my son from them; he has to face them. But it's hard to try to stop your son from, say, blaspheming, when your husband does it! You just have to keep on and on and standing your ground and explaining what you believe in."

Mandy experienced serious problems at home. "My husband's eldest daughter came to live with us six years ago. She had lots of problems and I found her very secular and holding worldly views. It was very difficult and I felt the need to counteract them, especially as my son had a more Christian perspective."

Some parents, however, have worked through this dilemma. Anne says that her husband "has always been extremely helpful. We are able to discuss and support each other with the children. Our morals and ethics do not always agree, but we are able to discuss them."

Kay seems to have worked through many of these problems and now finds that her sons respect her faith. "Our two sons (ages twenty-two and twenty) are loving and accepting, although their tastes in television and music are often contradictory to my beliefs. They do, however, change the channel or turn it off if I am part of the viewing or listening group."

I have noticed an interesting feature when comparing survey forms from wives with those from husbands. Almost all the Christian mothers told of difficulties they have found in raising children when their husband does not share their faith. In comparison, only two fathers referred to any kind of problem. Most said "None" when they answered this question, while one said "None, unless the children are indoctrinated," and another said that he had a problem because "... my wife's commitment to the church means she spends less time with my daughter." It seems that the men, in general, are oblivious to the tensions and frustrations experienced by their wives.

THE REACTIONS OF CHILDREN

Children who have to cope with continuous tensions at home because their parents are not united in the area of personal faith respond in various ways. In this section we explore some of their reactions.

A tendency to identify with one parent more than the other. When a child or adolescent loves and values both parents, yet finds that there is serious disagreement between them, he or she faces a dilemma. We have already seen that the youngster is likely to become confused if the position of both seems sensible and well-reasoned. How can children cope with a permanent situation they neither asked for nor like?

As the child grows, he or she will become more and more able to understand what is going on between the parents and what the real issues are. He or she will then be able to start the long process of coming to his or her own conclusions. In the case of parents who do not see eye to eye over the Christian faith, the young person himself or herself will have to decide whether or not to explore it more deeply.

Pauline's three eldest children, all daughters, tend to identify with their mother over matters of faith. "My husband is always very negative. He says when you are dead, that's it, so you have to make the best of now. He says that people only become Christians as an insurance policy for eternity. I constantly give the positive side and the girls support me."

Sadly, Liz's children are not at the same point. "Our children are now adults, but they have been affected by many factors including my husband's anti-Christianity stance. He was a very heavy drinker in the past, with a violent and nasty streak, and was very unpredictable in his behavior... I brought up the children myself. He does not drink any longer, but because of an injury, he cannot work and so relies on painkillers that have produced the same symptoms as drink did in the past. Praise God, he has received counseling for this and is attempting to reduce the amount he takes. Neither of our sons attends church. The older one professes no belief in God, and the younger is backslidden. They both look to their father's example and see God as an irrelevance."

Younger children face a different problem. Without the mental capacity to work through the issues, and finding that trying to straddle the position of both parents is sometimes very painful and uncomfortable, they find only one option open to them. This is to identify more with one parent than the other. Their selection is probably more instinctive than rational.

One wife told me that she has her children in her care "almost 99 percent of the time," although, she says, "we both share them and look after them." Her husband is out at work for much of the day. In her situation, therefore, she has most direct dealings with them and therefore probably has the closer relationship. Maybe it is for this reason that in many cases where mother is a Christian and father is not, the children happily accompany mother to church while father stays home alone.

As they grow older, boys especially start to notice the role model being provided by their father. If he is not a committed Christian and does not attend church, a boy may well decide that now he wants to stay at home with dad instead of going off to "boring old church." In making this decision he will, of course, fall foul of his mother. In circumstances like this, pleasing both parents at once is not possible.

One wife reported that her son "doesn't see why he has to go to church when Daddy doesn't," while another explains how her husband embarrasses the children. "He swears and does things that I feel are dishonest. He has been physically violent in the past and the children have been involved and heard him threaten to kill himself and us along with him. They are embarrassed by his behavior when they bring friends home." Children usually have difficulty rationalizing this kind of situation and experience feelings of guilt and shame. They tend to think that somehow it is their fault and may well need reassurance.

Sadness. Children normally want to please their parents at least some of the time. (Parents wish it was all of the time!) Children like being praised. Most get a real kick from being told by both parents how well they have done. It can cause them distress, therefore, to discover that in some cases they may not be able to earn sincere praise from both parents at the same time.

The time may come, for instance, when a teenager who earlier made a sincere, if fairly private, commitment of his or her life to Jesus Christ, now wants to be confirmed or baptized by immersion as a believer. Mother, as a Christian, is overjoyed. Father, maybe an agnostic, fails to see what all the fuss is about. He learns quite quickly that a special ceremony will take place on a given date and everyone expects him to be there. The prospect of this does not excite him. Indeed, if he should be in bed with flu at the time, it would be a welcome alternative. People who have chosen not to attend church as a regular activity find the prospect of having to do so for a special occasion quite frightening.

This attitude, while honest, can be a definite dampener on the joy and enthusiasm of a young person being baptized or confirmed. Of course, no one would encourage a parent in this situation to display false happiness and delight. However, looking at things from the young person's perspective, we can see how they may be sad to see genuine support and encouragement coming from only one of their parents.

Upset. Children learn that serious disagreements within a family are painful. Like other family members, they can suffer considerable emotional pain when an argument breaks out and anger, grief, and distress spread around the house. A little spark about church, or what is or is not acceptable within the household, can ignite a mighty blaze. It is one thing for the parents to disagree; it is something else for their children to find themselves entangled in the fracas that follows. In these situations, children often feel guilty.

It is probably true that few things upset children and teenagers as much as watching and listening to their parents participating in a serious confrontation. They find themselves in a situation that they can neither control nor influence. My research suggests that the Christian faith of one partner does not seem to provoke endless disputes in most families. Where it does, however, it often brings considerable distress to the youngsters on the sidelines, who may not be very forgiving.

Resentment toward religious faith. If children experience a succession of unpleasant incidents which revolve largely around one issue, they may become skeptical about that issue. If, because one parent is a committed Christian and the other is not, they repeatedly argue and disagree about religion, the children may come to their own conclusions about it. They would base these on what they have seen and heard many times. "If God and church have this effect on people's relationships," they may say, "I will skip religion in my life."

No one can blame young people for coming to such a conclusion, which is only based on what they have witnessed at close quarters. Their resentment is directed toward what they perceive to be the root cause of friction in their home.

Emma is a teenager with one parent who is a Christian and one who is not. She seems to resent the effect of this problem on her family. "I used to go to Sunday school and church outings, but I stopped going because I found it boring. My mom goes out to church four times a week at least, and Dad gets angry at this. I don't mind my mom being a Christian, but sometimes she gets a bit overpowering, talking about God all the time and why I need to be good."

Arnold, now middle-aged, grew up in a family like this and also seems to resent Christianity. "My mother kept forcing the idea on my brother and me. It led to heated discussions sometimes, which resulted in difficulties. I felt sorry for my father, who appeared to be left out of church activities."

THE EFFECT OF CONFLICT

In the same way that soldiers often return from the field of battle wounded emotionally, if not physically, so anyone who lives in a domestic war zone for any length of time will have a price to pay. Sadly, children are among the most vulnerable.

Before we explore the effect conflict in the home has on children, we need to discuss a question asked by D.W. Winnicott.

What is the normal child like? Does he just eat and grow and smile sweetly? No, that is not what he is like. A normal child, if he has confidence in father and mother, pulls out all the stops. In the course of time he tries out his power to disrupt, to destroy, to frighten, to wear down, to waste, to wangle, and to appropriate.... If the home can stand up to all the child can do to disrupt it, he settles down to play; but business first, the tests must be made, and especially so if there is some doubt as to the stability of the parental set-up and the home.[1]

Children look for a secure framework in which to live, and become uncertain of where they stand if they live in a home where conflict is commonplace. The friction, of course, can be due to anything that comes between people who share life together. The effect on the children, however, is the same whether it is the alleged unfaithfulness of the husband or wife that is being argued about, or the fact that one of them believes in Jesus Christ while the other does not. For a moment we will explore the effects of conflict on children without constant reference to the main subject matter of this book.

Children become unsettled if they have to face circumstances which are emotionally demanding and stressful, and which they have not experienced before. Generally, however, they are used to their own homes, whatever they are like. As Rosemary Wells reminds us,

> They *know* dad gets angry when drunk; they *know* mom is often out when they get home from school; they are *used* to their parents only talking through the children—that's their home. Only if dad threatens to leave, or mom talks of abandoning them, is real security at stake.[2]

Having said this, we need to ask what we may do to our children if we conclude that fighting is perfectly natural and acceptable, so long as we do not go too far and say things that are excessive. Parents with impressionable children at home have a responsibility to protect them from as much marital conflict as possible, certainly when it is not the children's immediate concern.

When we subject children to serious domestic tension, we run the risk of destroying the secure framework they need if they are to become emotionally balanced adults. Steve Hepden says that a child who, among other problems, has unhappy parents is in danger of feeling rejected. He also teaches that "religious pressure on children from parents can cause legalism, traditionalism, and inflexibility which will lead to self-rejection."[3]

D.W. Winnicott describes what may happen if a child fails to find the security he needs at home.

> The child whose home fails to give a feeling of security looks outside his home for the four walls; he still has hope, and he looks to grandparents, uncles and aunts, friends of the family, school. He seeks an external stability without which he may go mad... Often a child gets from relations and school what he missed in his own actual home.[4]

When parents find themselves caught up in serious domestic and marital conflict, they may feel that simply to survive to fight another day is a major accomplishment, and so it may be. Yet even in such dire circumstances, surely they cannot overlook the children whom they brought into the world and who are dependent on them for so much.

Parents may feel that if they are both there and they are providing materially and physically for the children, that is enough. From the children's perspective, it is probably grossly inadequate. They know something is missing, but do not know what.

Children are at risk emotionally in situations where parents fail to resolve their differences and the problems continue. They also suffer when parents fail to have respect for each other's opinions and feelings, and where a harmonious resolution, therefore, is made more difficult.

Children are much too important to be disadvantaged because of problems in the home that very possibly could be reduced, if not fully resolved. When there is a link between the problems in the marriage and the Christian faith, it somehow seems even more tragic that innocent children may be experiencing harm. If so, it is even more vital that something positive should be done. We will discuss possible courses of action in the next chapter.

CHAPTER SEVEN

How Can You Help Your Children?

The world is a tough environment in which children have to grow up. It becomes tougher if they have to face additional pressures such as parents who disagree fundamentally about something as important as Christian belief.

This chapter recognizes that you, as the Christian parent, are likely to be the principal reader of this book. It will encourage you to think through what you can do for your children as they grow up in a situation that is more demanding than you would wish. We will focus on a combination of spiritual and practical issues as we answer the question: "How can you best help your children in this situation?" We will explore three ways.

EXPLANATIONS

Children may not have lived for many years, but they can be very perceptive. Nothing works better with children who have an endless supply of important questions than a steady stream of straight answers. Trying to put them off is seldom successful.

When their parents have differing views about God, Christianity, and church that sometimes create conflict in the home, children need to talk about it. Let us identify some areas of discussion that they will appreciate.

The truth. Children may not always tell the truth themselves, but they expect adults to be straight with them. If their parents have a tendency to fight over a given issue, they like to know what it is. Rosemary Wells explains why this is important.

> [A survey done by a British TV station] found the strongest factor throughout their conversations with children was that parents seldom talk with them, involve them, allow them to be part of the family discussions. Children I have spoken with all want to know what is happening, and to feel their parents respect their wishes and recognize their needs. A child can sense when things are upset, and fantasies and anxieties will build up in a young mind which can cause far more damage than hearing the truth.[1]

The value of open and honest discussion is that misconceptions and unnecessary fears can be laid to rest quickly. What children sometimes imagine is often very much more sinister than the reality.

When problems in the family are largely over your personal faith that your husband does not share, explain this to the children with tact and sensitivity. It would be unfair to use this as a way of surreptitiously preaching the gospel at them, but you can simply explain what your faith means to you and why you are glad to be a Christian. You can then explain that their dad does not feel the same way about God, and may like to suggest that they discuss this issue, and the differences in your views, with him too.

At a time when you are seeking to explain a situation to your children, it is important that you are balanced and fair. It could rebound on you if you try to influence them to your view. They may remember what you say and harbor resentment that you appeared to be trying to manipulate them.

The timing is also important. Bedtime may appear to be the obvious time for intimate discussion, but it is likely to awaken the mind of a previously tired child. Not only is your child unlikely to sleep for a long time afterward, but he or she would have the disadvantage of not being able to ask supplementary questions right away. A better time for discussions like this may be, for instance, a Saturday morning.

Love. When children are in the thick of unsettling circumstances, what they need most of all is reassurance. One boy was given all the reassurance his parents could muster at a difficult time:

Asked by his teacher to write an essay about the most memorable event in his holidays, a boy of twelve wrote of the day his parents told him they were getting a divorce. They sat either side of him and each parent took one of his hands. His father spoke: "Son, we want you to be the first to know that mummy and I are separating. This may upset you, but the important thing to remember is that we both love you, and always will." The boy wrote that his father's eyes were filled with tears and his mother was openly crying. "We both love you," she echoed.[2]

While we all need to know that others love and appreciate us, children need this reassurance most. They also need to hear the same message again and again, particularly if they are in stressful circumstances. If your children are at all perturbed by any disagreements between your husband and yourself, tell them often how much you love and value them. They will appreciate it and it will go a long way to reassuring them that they really matter to you.

The gospel. We said earlier that when you give your children an explanation of your situation, it would be unwise to use it as an excuse to preach the Good News of Jesus to them. Despite this new heading, this counsel still stands.

You may find occasions arise when your child asks you a direct question about your faith, what you believe and why. This puts you in a predicament. If you can give a clear and straight answer, you would be dishonest not to do so, but if you directly share the gospel with your child and your husband finds out, he may charge you with indoctrination.

This is Stephanie's problem. She says that her major problem at home in this area is "letting the children learn more about the Bible and answering their questions about Christ, without making my husband feel they are being, to use his word, 'indoctrinated.'"

This is a dilemma faced frequently by thousands of Christians. Madeleine recalls how her husband opposed her teaching her two girls about Christianity when they were younger. "To begin with [he opposed it] angrily and explicitly, and then, later, implicitly, by snide remarks and belittling."

This raises an important question. Who am I most accountable to when the Bible tells me to talk about Jesus, and my husband disapproves of me telling our children? I cannot and must not make up your mind for you, but you may feel that there are occasions when you can gently explain to them how much God loves them, and how much he wants them to love him in return.

While recognizing the delicacy of your situation at home, if an appropriate opportunity arises, you may be able to explain what Jesus said about the relationships of those who put their trust in him (Mt 10:21-22; 34-38). He never suggested that the whole world would follow him enthusiastically; on the contrary, he taught that opposition, misunderstanding, and rejection will be familiar to many of his disciples. What is happening in your home may be a fulfillment of these words, and it is probably best if your children understand this.

Your reasons. Policy disagreements often cause the most trouble at home. Julie states her main problem as the discrepancy between her views and her husband's about what TV programs and movies are acceptable for their son to see. "He appears to be more laid back about what our son watches," she says.

At times like this, when a child feels that one parent's treatment at home is unfair, you may need to give an explanation. He may say, "But if Dad were here he would let me see it," and that may be true. If you have an instinctive uneasiness about a particular show, however, and feel the need to insist the child does not see it, you must be able to explain your reasons adequately, whether your child accepts them happily or not.

The same is true of more serious issues. You must be able to explain, for instance, why you do not accept that it is right for couples to live together unless they are married, or for sexual intercourse to take place outside marriage. You must be able to account, as Peter put it, "for the hope that you have" (1 Pet 3:15).

Christianity is rational and there are good reasons why God has instructed us to live the way he has. You cannot, of course, easily impose Christian ethics and morals on those who have not accepted Jesus as Lord, but you must, at least, be able to explain why you hold the views you do. For you to be able to help your children, it is important for you to be able to express yourself and explain your position in these four areas we have discussed.

ENCOURAGEMENT

Barnabas, a member of the early church in Jerusalem, brought great encouragement to the fellowship (see Acts 4:36-37, 9:27, 13:43-49, 14:14-18, 15:35).

To have a ministry of encouragement in a home where there is stress and conflict could be enormously enriching. Paul tells us that we should "eagerly desire the greater gifts" (1 Cor 12:31), and maybe in your circumstances the gift of encouragement would be one of the greatest to receive.

Let us consider a number of ways in which you can encourage your children if they are finding life hard because they are caught up in problems between you and your husband over faith.

To talk. We noted earlier how the minds of youngsters can be unhelpfully creative when they suspect a crisis but are unsure what is really going on. Maybe the best thing a parent can do in these circumstances is to encourage them to talk about it.

Naturally, most parents prefer their children to choose to talk their problems through with them. However, especially as youngsters grow older, many children feel far more comfortable discussing personal and serious matters with someone other than their parents, maybe someone right outside the family. Never be hurt by this; it is very normal."[3] What matters most is that children and young people who live in unsettling circumstances have someone accessible with whom they can talk when they have the need.

If the time comes, and a child or young person chooses to open up to his or her parents, it is important for them to listen to how their child *feels*, without interrupting or correcting. Such self-disciplined listening may not come easily or naturally, but it is vital for two reasons. First, because the child needs to know that he or she is being taken seriously and treated with respect as a person. Second, in order to reassure the child that this is a safe and productive course of action to take when future problems arise.

To spend time with their father. A danger exists if you and your husband have different understandings of life because you have a living faith in Jesus that he does not share. Because you urgently want your children to become Christians too, you may be overeager to protect them by being nearby as much as possible. You may even try to stop your husband influencing their development too much if you know that his views and yours do not always match.

At this point you have to decide what are the greatest hazards for your children. Your husband might, for instance, take the children to see movies about which you would have serious reservations. However, your children need the input into their lives that only their father can give. For their balanced emotional development they need to spend as much time with him as they do with you.

Let us go further. Virtually all children spend more time with their mothers than with their fathers. In order to help redress the balance, why not encourage your husband to take each of the children out on his own? They do not need to go anywhere expensive—a walk around your local area may be enough. What matters is that your children can speak to their father and have a developing relationship with him.

If you begin to get uneasy about any unhelpful influences that you think the children may be exposed to at this time, there are two possibilities open to you. First, you can mention it gently to your husband. Second, you can pray. You can do no better than to entrust your children to God's protection. Whether you like it or not, they will come across all sorts of unhelpful influences at school, if nowhere else. Simply ask God to take care of them and trust that he will help them make sound judgments about what they see and hear.

To pray. Even if you are the only born-again believer in your home, you are not the only person who has access to God in prayer. Sometimes I encounter people who never go near a church and clearly have never made a commitment to follow Christ, yet they tell me how they pray every night before they go to bed. Who can say that God does not hear and answer them? Knowing that God is by nature gracious, merciful, and loving, we dare not conclude that God ignores their prayers if they are sincere.

Apply this to your children and the problems they get involved in at home because only one of their parents is an active Christian. If you can see that they are experiencing pain and confusion, why not suggest that they talk to God about it? Without being in the least disloyal to your husband, you can say that this is precisely what you do. You can explain how helpful you find it to be able to express your feelings to someone you know understands. If you experience it personally, you can testify to the peace and strength God gives you once you have spoken with him in this way.

Jill tries to help her thirteen-year-old daughter who, she says, "used to come to church from the age of five years until about a year ago. She does pray and we talk about different problems that occur in her life and I pray with her about them. Jesus always solves them for her."

To relate to nearby Christian families. Let us assume that, more than anything else, you want your husband and children to come to know Jesus Christ personally. Ideally the children will respond to Christ before they leave home. How can you help this to happen?

You may be able to encourage a relationship to develop between your family and another family in which the husband has made a commitment to Christ, and maybe some of the children are Christians too. Naturally, this will only happen if you and the other wife relate well, and if others in the two families have things in common.

If the families get along fairly well on a personal level, it could help your children to see the differences that Christ makes in another home. Of course, the other family must be sensitive and careful not to exert any spiritual pressure. If, however, your husband or children start to ask them questions about God or church, they can answer them.

To go to church on Sundays. While children are influenced by a wide variety of things, their parents' example is among the most significant. If one parent attends church and the other does not, they will naturally find it hard to decide which role model to follow. As they grow up they will realize how few of their contemporaries attend church, and may question seriously whether they should go anymore.

At this point you have an important part to play in helping them. If you are too directive and domineering, especially as they grow older, it is likely to be counter-productive, but some gentle encouragement could help them a lot. The older they are, the more important it is to explain *why* it is worth being part of a church. If they argue that *your* church is boring or unsuitable, you may have to accept this as their perception and encourage them to find another that suits them more.

Whatever the outcome, probably what matters most is that you exercise some leadership as a parent when your children find it tough. Even if they ignore your counsel, it is important for you to be aware that God knows that you tried. It is important also for them that you did not desert them to work things out alone when they were struggling.

Mary has tried to do this with her seventeen-year-old son. "My son attended Sunday school until he was nine, and then got to the stage where it was a struggle to get him to attend. Since then I have encouraged him to attend church. He does come with me sometimes, but shows no interest as none of his friends are churchgoers. My husband just tells him to make up his own mind."

To develop friendships within the church. When children and young people have a period of doubt or difficulty, it is often the relationships with their peers that encourage them to keep going to church. Many an adolescent has stayed at church, and later been converted, because of strong friendships within the church youth group.

Parents cannot select friends for their offspring, of course, but they can influence, even minimally, the choices that their children make. What is clear is that their children, humanly at least, are far more likely to enter a personal relationship with Jesus Christ if they are integrated into spiritual church-based youth activities, than if their friendships are generally outside the church.

Making friends with other young people in the church could be very beneficial for your child, especially if some of them come from Christian homes. If your child visits their homes from time to time, he or she will see how a Christian family functions. It will have its imperfections, of course, but if your son or daughter has become a Christian, it could help him or her to understand how important it is to find a Christian partner when the time comes to settle down.

EXAMPLE

All of us need to see competent demonstrations of what we are aiming to master ourselves, and our children are no exception. They will identify their own role models as they grow up, and allow these people, whether living, dead, or fictional, to influence their lives. Our task now is to explore ways in which you as a Christian parent can affect the development of your children positively by being an example they can follow.

Living the Christian life despite difficulties. If life is comparatively stable and straightforward, most Christians do not find it too hard to follow Christ reasonably loyally. The true depth of our faith is tested when problems arise. The way in which we allow our faith to affect our lives in times of difficulty will demonstrate how real it is. For some Christians, problems rarely go away, and certainly this may be the case with some wives whose husbands do not share their faith. The pressure rarely drops as long as the wife takes her relationship with Jesus seriously.

Ros' husband will not attend church with her, but she is conscious of the influence she can exert on him and their three children by her example. "I do not 'push' my husband into doing things he does not want to. I hope, eventually, he will learn by my example. I also make sure he feels he is important to me (which he is!) and that after eighteen years I am not looking for anyone to replace him."

Our children cannot fail to notice how each partner responds to the other when they disagree over anything to do with faith. They may know what triggers arguments and bad feeling long before it dawns on their parents. They will certainly come to their own conclusions about who provokes whom and what the contentious issues are.

The more the qualities of Jesus blossom in you in demanding circumstances, the more you will help your children to understand how to become and live as Christians. Seeing Christianity work as it should in the life of someone close to them cannot fail to make an enormous impact on them.

Being sensitive and conciliatory. During his ministry on earth, Jesus had a lot of contact with ordinary people, some of them with very great needs. As we read the gospel records of his meetings with them, we see the love and compassion he had for people. He even cared about the religious leaders who displayed anger and jealousy toward him, although their attacks on him intensified as time went on.

Perhaps your situation at home is demanding. We have already identified the problems caused in some homes when a Christian wife wants to play a full part in the life of her church, including being there every Sunday. If her husband appreciates a different way of life, it so easily leads to contention and strife.

Angela describes a problem with parenting that she and her husband have that is caused by her being a Christian when he is not. "It occurs on Sundays," she says, "when I want to take the children to church and he wants to take them to his parents."

Children can find tension wearisome and may develop sympathies one way or the other. What they will appreciate and value in both parents is an openness to see the other's point of view and, on occasions at least, a willingness to be flexible in order to show love and respect for the partner's perspective. When the Christian wife takes the initiative and behaves this way toward her husband, it reinforces the truth that Christianity is about love, understanding, and reconciliation, rather than harsh and rigid legalism.

Angela feels she is being "held back" because she cannot always attend church on a Sunday or other occasions. "I have to balance the family with God," she says, but she is delighted that her husband now encourages her to go to church and has begun to read some of her Christian books.

Upholding biblical moral standards. In the age in which we live, people are often encouraged to do what seems best in any situation, not necessarily what is right or wrong. Indeed, many people believe it is better to play down rigid moral absolutes and let individuals plot their own courses through life. Not surprisingly, this approach creates problems for many Christians because of the definitive truth of God they discover in the Bible.

It is now unfashionable in many Western cultures to have and to live by clear moral standards. Christians today live in an increasingly secular and materialistic age, where a lifestyle that emulates Jesus is more and more at odds with mainstream society. Our children are growing up at a time when right and wrong, good and bad are outdated concepts. They are encouraged simply to do whatever appeals to them, with almost no moral absolutes to guide them.

God calls those of us who have made a commitment to

Christ to be humble, righteous, holy, filled with the Holy Spirit, and submissive to our Father in heaven. He challenges us to live according to his standards and levels of behavior, although these may be different from those of our families. This is not easy and leads inevitably to conflict at times, but God has called us to be witnesses for him in that hardest of all places to live out the Christian faith, the family home.

Pauline confesses that she struggles with some things in particular. "I find it hard to come to terms with the fact that my eldest son married a divorced woman and that my younger son (who says he is a Christian) lives with his girlfriend and their daughter. My husband can't see anything wrong in it."

Your example at home, however, is of the utmost importance in God's plan for your family. If you seem to have a greater sense of contentment and fulfillment in life as you try to live by God's moral standards, it will have an effect on them, whether they tell you or not.

Getting outside help for yourself. A common human tendency is for us to give the impression that we are coping with life and its pressures when in fact we are struggling. This is largely because it would be embarrassing to admit to failure. It matters to us enormously how others perceive us.

Some people feel that there is a stigma attached to asking for help from outside agencies. As a pastor, I have known many people who declined help not only from me, but also from my wife or another caring person, either because they found it too embarrassing a prospect or because they could not face up to the reality of their problem. This is something that is worth trying to overcome.

Two things are important here. First, we must receive the help we need at the time we need it, and, secondly, our children must see that we do. Setting an example for them to follow is almost as important as receiving the help ourselves. They need to see that a realistic approach to life, where we openly accept we have problems and face up to them, is by far the best way to live.

It is only when we recognize our problems and pray about them realistically that we draw on God and his resources. Older children in particular need to learn from our example how to face *their* problems. Ideally, they need to see us combining the spiritual and practical approaches: praying, on the one hand, and consulting our church leaders or other counselors on the other. Our goal is to act responsibly ourselves and help our children to be more prepared for their futures.

We expect our children to have many years ahead of them. We know that their lives, both in this world and eternity, will be enriched most of all if they have a personal relationship with Jesus Christ. Whether they recognize it or not, they need him more than anything or anyone else. The best thing that we can do for them is to help them discover him for themselves.

It would be easier if they were growing up in a spiritually united home, but, for the time being at least, this cannot be. This inevitably means that a lot of pressure falls on you as their sole Christian parent, and you will always find this role demanding and strenuous.

The only way that you will be able to help them on a spiritual level is if you stay close to the Lord yourself. When you have a close relationship with Jesus and the power of his Holy Spirit is flowing to and through you, you will have the capacity to help your children spiritually. If you seek to live for him at home and in your family relationships, you will provide God with an opportunity to speak to your children. This is surely what God asks you to do for him and them.

PART FOUR

All About Your Church

CHAPTER EIGHT

How Can Your Church Help You?

Now that we have taken time to consider the situation from your perspective and that of your family, we come finally to reflect on the vital part your local church has to play in your life. While this chapter is primarily written for you, I am aware that, even if you find the suggestions helpful, you may not be able to do much about implementing them in your church. Therefore, this chapter is intended both for you and your church leaders, who should be able to influence the direction in which your church moves and the ministry it offers. You may want to lend this book to them when you have finished reading it, so that they can see how your church could help you more. Before we reflect on this in practical terms, however, we need to think about God's intentions for every church.

Ask a few of your neighbors what they feel about church, and you may find they give negative reactions. Sadly, many people have had bad experiences and view the church either with disdain or as utterly irrelevant. Of all the groupings in society that draw like-minded people together, maybe the Christian church is the most misunderstood and unappreciated. I hope your experience of church is more positive than this.

Jesus first used the word "church" of those who followed him. Simon, the former fisherman, correctly identified Jesus as "the Christ, the Son of the living God" (Mt 16:16). He told

Simon that he was renaming him "Peter" because "on this rock I will build my church" (Mt 16:18). Largely because of his recognition of Jesus as the long-awaited Jewish Messiah, Peter would have a significant part to play in building the community of those who chose to follow Christ.

His key role became apparent on the day of Pentecost when the Holy Spirit filled the disciples of Jesus (Acts 2:4). When the crowd accused them of being drunk, Peter immediately took the initiative and spoke out. Prompted by the Holy Spirit, he not only refuted the charge, but also proclaimed powerfully the truth about Jesus Christ (Acts 2:14-36). God used Peter's words, and many in the crowd came under conviction of sin and pleaded to know how they could find peace with God. After he told them to repent and believe, three thousand people became followers of Jesus, and those who lived locally formed the first Christian church in Jerusalem.

Luke tells us what church life was like in those early days. The Christians met to worship, to be taught, to share fellowship, to pray, and to eat together. They supported each other practically and developed deep bonds of love and commitment to one another as fellow disciples of Christ. It is no surprise that God blessed them by drawing a succession of people to Christ through their ministry (Acts 2:42-47).

These verses show us what God intended to be key ingredients in the life and ministry of any church in every era and culture. In other parts of the New Testament we find further insights into different Christian churches. These give us an even broader and more comprehensive picture.

THE CHURCH AS GOD INTENDED

A family. Paul refers to God's family as being "in heaven and on earth" (Eph 3:15). Those on earth are "sons of God through faith in Christ Jesus" (Gal 3:26) and have "the full rights of sons" and are his "heirs" (Gal 4:5-7). He says that all disciples of Christ have ceased to be "foreigners and aliens" and have become, by God's power, "fellow-citizens with God's people and members of God's household" (Eph 2:19). God's work is to transform in a remarkable way the lives of ordinary human beings who put their trust and faith in his Son.

Paul expects Christians who are part of the same church to live together in unity. He believes that every part of God's family on earth should experience harmony, and is distressed to find the Christians in Corinth quarrelling among themselves about which church leader they support most (1 Cor 3:1-5). He is disturbed to hear about believers in Galatia "biting and devouring each other" and refers to hatred and discord as "acts of the sinful nature" (Gal 5:15; 19-21). Paul sees it as totally inconsistent for Christians to say they are God's family on earth, and yet live as if God had not worked in their lives at all.

Jesus describes the relationships he expects to see between Christians. "Love each other as I have loved you," he told the twelve (Jn 15:12). He wants his family to be bonded together by the same powerful force that binds them to him. Those in any generation who are part of Christ's church should experience his love and acceptance as it flows to them through other believers.

A flock. Not only does God intend the church to be an accepting and loving community, but also to provide care for its members. Jesus reintroduced the imagery of Psalm 23 when he spoke of himself as "the good shepherd" (Jn 10:11, 14). As the guide, provider, and protector of those who follow him, he accepts full responsibility for them. He wants them to understand that his love for them is so great that he will pay even the ultimate price to protect them (Jn 10:15). It is important to him that they know he is there because he has great power and authority. He wants them to feel reassured and safe.

A further confirmation that the Christian church is to resemble a flock of sheep comes in Peter's first letter. He appeals to the elders in the church to "be shepherds of God's flock that is under your care" and "examples to the flock" (1 Pt 5:2-3). Our churches are to be centers of caring where all who are part of them feel the support and care, both of the leaders and others in the fellowship. Without delay leaders need to introduce improvements, because recent research suggests that many people leave churches at least partly because they feel that they do not belong.[1]

A body. In addition to churches being united, loving, and caring communities of God's people, the New Testament also shows us that they have a function to fulfill. God entrusts the born-again, Spirit-filled disciples of Christ in every church with special gifts and ministries. He wants them to use these under the Holy Spirit's guidance to build up the church and help it become mature (Eph 4:11-13). The New Testament identifies many gifts (Rom 12:6-8; 1 Cor 12:8-10, 28; Eph 4:11; 1 Pt 4:10-11), but these lists are not intended to be exclusive. God has the capacity to provide any gift needed to build up his church at any time.

Paul is careful to explain to the Corinthian Christians the way that these various gifts should interrelate. The "same Spirit" gives them all and the "same Lord" directs them all (1 Cor 12:4-5). They are the "many parts" which "form one body" (v. 12) and all have an equally vital role to play (vv. 22-24). God's intention is that "there should be no division in the body, but that its parts should have equal concern for each other" (v. 25). If Christians use all the gifts entrusted to the body as God intends, they will complement one another and allow the body to function effectively.

The concept of any Christian being an inactive member of a

church was inconceivable to Paul. He took it for granted that every disciple of Christ would want to serve his or her Master in a specific way. Not only must Christians do this to show that they are deeply grateful that Jesus has accepted them into his family, but it is also important for them to be integrated fully into the body. For anyone to feel a full part of a church, they need to have a part to play in it.

In these three sections, we have covered part of the New Testament teaching about the church. We need now to see how local churches should be applying this so that wives whose husbands do not share their faith are helped and supported in circumstances that may be difficult.

THE HELP THAT IS NEEDED

Understanding. In the light of Jesus' words that his disciples should love one another, each church should provide a caring environment where love and acceptance are prominent. Those who are members should be so aware of their own areas of vulnerability and weakness that they are understanding and compassionate when faced with the sensitive pastoral problems of others.

Wives whose husbands do not share their faith need to feel accepted, cared for, and understood by their church. This does not always happen. "M.J." is on record as saying, "I feel my church has let me down. I don't doubt for one minute that they care... but they just didn't seem to understand."[2] How can a church show empathy?

Churches should recognize that wives with uncommitted husbands need loving prayer support, because of the extra pressure they often experience at home. The wives need to know that many in their church, including the leaders, realize that they do not have the same freedom to participate in church life as others. They need reassurance that this is not frowned on or perceived as a lack of commitment.

Donna was criticized because she could not get to every meeting of her small group. "My small group leader made pointed comments to *other people*, who then reported back to me about people who do not regularly attend the group." Sandra gives us an insight into her church relationships. "One or two are very understanding, but unless you are in the same situation it is hard to understand the 'two way' pull. Some are less than understanding when I can't always join in things."

Churches need to provide a caring environment where people with many kinds of difficulties can come to find acceptance and understanding from those whom Christ is filling with compassion. When Christians make time for each other, they can experience mutual support that strengthens and reassures them. Wives with uncommitted husbands need this especially.

Support and encouragement. Having lived for many years as a Christian with a husband who did not share her faith, Linda Davis is unhappy at the way that women in this situation can be perceived, both at church and by themselves.

> It is time for the Body of Christ to realize that the Christian wife of an unbeliever is not a second-class citizen in the Church. She is a woman whom God has called to a noble and difficult ministry. Wives of unbelievers must stop regarding themselves as failures incapable of getting their husbands saved, and instead see themselves as selected saints, chosen to represent Christ to their husbands in the most intimate of relationships—marriage. And it is time for us all to acknowledge that being the wife of an unsaved husband is not a sin but, in fact, an honorable calling."[3]

Later, the same writer says that she doubts "that even physical widowhood makes a woman feel as rejected and inadequate as does 'spiritual widowhood'—the state of being married to one who is spiritually dead. The spiritual widow receives no flowers or sympathy cards. She simply grieves in silence for a union that never was."[4]

Such a graphic description reveals the extent to which wives in this situation need support from their church which they do not always receive. One wife says, "Some Christians are too busy and shut me out when I would like their fellowship."[5] Anne agrees, saying, "I don't feel I get that much support, although the situation is prayed for by my small group. It would be nice if people asked you to sit with them when you walked into church alone, instead of feeling as if you're latching on. The main reason I often don't attend events is that I hate going alone. Perhaps the church could put people like me in touch with others in the same position."

Fiona endorses this. "I would like to be involved in a prayer group where people like myself can pray together for our partners. I feel most churches are geared more to couples... and I often feel 'second class' because I am on my own. Our church leadership is made up of couples (not that I want to be one of the leaders) but it shows me that you are more accepted when your partner is with you."

Ruth's experience is hard and painful too. "I get prayer support from a few close friends, a small prayer chain, and a small group. At times I have received well-meaning sympathy about my problems, but, to be honest, it has only depressed me. I would like people to ask me how I am and not if my husband has been saved yet. Sometimes they tell me how quickly their partner got saved after presenting the gospel to him or her for only a couple of months."

Such statements suggest that there is room for improvement in some churches. A concept that others could borrow from a church with which I am familiar is the Family Life Festival. Focused on the Bible's teaching about family issues, the church used a wide range of different events for a whole month to encourage everyone in the church family. Wives whose husbands have not yet become Christians could receive help from such a program, although they need year-round support and encouragement too.

Sophie says that she receives this. "I get a lot of support from my church and I am aware that people pray for my husband. We are always asked as a couple to church social events. My Christian friends often give me words of encouragement and ask me to send him their love or say 'hello.'"

Prayer. Many Christian wives testify that the most significant kind of help they receive is when others pray for them and their partner. Linda says, "I get a lot of support and I know a lot of people are praying for my husband." Irene receives encouragement from five of the young people in her church who pray for her and her husband regularly. Anne has appreciated the "practical and emotional support from many in the past three years" and "much prayer." Janice says, "I know a few friends who always pray for non-Christian husbands to know the Lord."

While it is very encouraging for a wife to know that others are praying for her husband, she also needs prayer support herself. Marion says she receives this "from other Christian friends who are in the same position." Many other wives who responded to my survey, however, felt they needed more personal prayer back-up.

For some, a fellowship group for women in this situation is their ideal choice. Linda filled in my questionnaire, reporting that "I have spoken to my minister today about setting up a group for Christians whose partners do not share their faith." Maybe more Christian wives in our churches would get greater support if they took initiatives like this.

What I discovered from the questionnaires returned to me is that only 2 percent of them contained any reference to groups of this kind where wives with husbands who do not share their faith can meet together. The explanation for this may be simple. Most church leaders are male, and as these leaders usually take the initiative for new groups in a church, this is one that they tend to overlook. If they became aware of the genuine help such a group could give, many leaders would probably set one up in their churches without delay.

My research suggests that in many cases the wives concerned would be very appreciative. If such groups existed, however, some wives would be unable to attend because of other responsibilities. Each wife must have her needs for prayer met according to her circumstances and preferences. Some will value their friends praying for them in their absence; others will need to be part of a group if they can. As far as possible, what matters is that each wife knows that she is being committed to God's care regularly by other caring Christians.

Pastoral counsel. Every Christian who belongs to a church is privileged to be part of a community of people with wide experiences of God and life. As they meet together, God can encourage and strengthen them all.

When Christians do this, those with specific and continuing problems can share experiences with others, especially those whose circumstances are similar. This exchange enhances everyone's understanding and helps them to see areas where they may experience conflict or misunderstanding in the future. If these problems then occur, they will know that others have already experienced similar difficulties before and will not think of themselves as unique.

It is important that a Christian wife, who might otherwise feel isolated and neglected, knows that there are people to whom she can turn if she feels the need. She may choose to go to one of her church leaders, or to one of the wives whose circumstances are similar to her own. What matters is that she knows that someone is readily available who can both empathize with her and encourage her.

HOW CHURCHES CAN HELP

How can a church best help wives whose husbands do not share their faith? Certain characteristics will enhance its ministry to these women.

A nonjudgmental attitude. Christianity is a faith that demands to be taken seriously. Because Jesus Christ made enormous sacrifices by becoming man and suffering death on a Roman cross, we cannot view lightly the call he issues to follow him. Many churches stress the absolute importance of loyal and dedicated service to Christ and his church. Often, however, churches seem to measure commitment by attendance at Christian events. This means that if someone is consistently present, others perceive them as being committed. Those who are rarely there are assumed to have only a shallow commitment. Intentionally or not, people make judgments about the dedication of others to Christ and his church. This is dangerous.

In view of the delicate situation experienced by some Christian wives whose husbands do not share their faith, such a conclusion could be quite wrong. Kathleen's church does not judge her. "My church fellowship helps by accepting and understanding me in my situation. I know they love me, even though I'm often not at church,"[6] she says.

Angela is able to testify that she receives similar encouragement. "I receive a lot of support from my Christian friends, and they pray for my husband frequently. We have also been invited for a meal at the home of one of our elders, and my husband has accepted. Our leaders don't expect me to be as involved or attend church and other meetings as often as others. That relieves a great deal of pressure."

This approach shows respect for the words of Jesus, "Do not judge" (Mt 7:1), and allows a much healthier attitude toward others within the church. A church where people criticize each other constantly is bound to have many difficulties. Inevitably, people will come to incorrect conclusions about each other and rumors will be rife. God cannot work easily in a church like this.

A Christian wife and her uncommitted husband need a church that accepts them as they are. If the wife is able to bring him to social events or to a Christmas carol service, they must both be greeted sincerely. This is where Kay finds that problems begin. "When we attend functions together, my husband is sometimes treated as a 'celebrity' and made to feel different. People mean to be kind and welcoming, but they only make him feel different." This does not help.

On other occasions, when a wife has to attend alone, she needs to know that she will receive an equally warm welcome and not be made to feel guilty because she has left her husband at home. Wives in these circumstances have enough to cope with without feeling condemned by fellow Christians.

Provide "bridging" events. What is increasingly apparent to many churches is that their culture is vastly different from that of mainstream secular society. While Christians can hop back and forth from one to the other once they have been believers for a while, people who do not have a Christian background find that the language, style, and approach of churches are not relevant to them at all. Even if someone presents the Christian faith to them, often they do not understand it. When faced with theological jargon and spiritual concepts, they become baffled and conclude that this message cannot be relevant to them.

For this reason, God seems to be challenging churches today to consider carefully two things: the message they proclaim, and how they share it. During his ministry, Jesus preached God's Good News in a way that caused many to accept it. Many people also became Christians during the period of church history covered in the Acts of the Apostles.

Today, however, in Western Europe and the United States, at least, church attendance is falling. This suggests that the message of the gospel is not being communicated effectively.

Some churches are growing. Among these are a number who are willing to reconsider the way they function. Some have been influenced by Willow Creek Community Church near Chicago, which has grown enormously since it was founded in 1975. Over 20,000 now attend their weekend "seeker" services where the audience enjoys a presentation of the Christian gospel in a style that is both lively and relevant. Most churches meet for worship on Sundays, but Willow Creek holds its worship midweek so that weekends are free for people who are not yet Christians to attend its seeker events. Willow Creek puts seekers first.

This approach is being adopted in varying degrees by churches around the world. Where I serve as pastor, there have been times when a third of the audience at our monthly "Sunday Night Live" presentations has been made up of people who do not attend our worship services. We have also found it encouraging that, sometimes, uncommitted husbands of Christian wives have attended. The fact that there is a Christian event to which the wives can bring their husbands without fear of them being embarrassed helps them. The fact that the husbands come encourages the church.

Whether or not churches introduce Willow Creek-type seeker services is not important. It *is* important that churches develop "bridging" events to which Christian wives can feel more relaxed about bringing their husbands. Churches must make it as easy as possible for Christian wives and others to bring their unconverted relatives, friends, and neighbors to Christian events. These do not have to be overtly spiritual occasions when the gospel is preached. What matters is that bridges are being built between those who are not committed to Christ and those who are.

What kind of events are held is not the most important

thing. What is important is how people are treated when they have the courage to attend these functions. Wendy says that there are times when those in the church "may be too pushy, which makes my husband back off, even if he had been interested in attending a function. He likes his own space and does things very much in his own time." Sandra's problem is the same. "He feels that some are 'out to get me' and he runs even further away. Now he will not even come to social events."

Vicki's difficulty is that her church friends swamp her husband. "They're always *so nice* to him when he sees them that he finds it suffocating. He's a big, tough guy and isn't used to everyone smiling and doing favors." Churches must learn what kind of events to arrange, and what approach to use with their guests when they come.

The possibilities are endless. Social events like parties, suppers, hikes, and outings for whole families could prove very popular. These would not draw attention to the families where the husband and father is not yet a Christian, but would allow a wide range of people to meet and mix easily and naturally. Wives whose husbands do not normally accompany them to church could often find these events helpful and encouraging.

Be sensitive about financial giving. At a time when many churches are finding it increasingly hard to cope financially, leaders are having to emphasize more than ever the need for responsible giving by their members. This is necessary to pay all the costs of local ministry, as well as supporting national structures and mission work at home and abroad.

When treasurers and leaders explain the financial needs of a church to its members, they invariably declare that it will take both dedication and generosity on the part of *everyone* to reach the target. Rarely do they identify those to whom this applies more (because they are very well off) or less (because they live in difficult or delicate circumstances). Presumably they do this because they do not want to offend anyone unnecessarily.

This leaves some people, wives with uncommitted husbands among them, with feelings of hurt and guilt. They feel hurt because it seems obvious that the church does not understand their predicament. They also feel guilty because they do not have the capacity or freedom to give away very much money.

Sophie says, "I am not able to contribute as much as I would like to the church or other Christian organizations." Sandy is frustrated too. "I would give more money at church if I could," she says. "It was especially a concern when he was the sole earner and it was not his priority." Mandy says that her husband "found tithing very hard to understand."

Madeleine felt that she had to be financially secretive. "I kept a little money from my final salary to one side (he *hates* this) because I wanted a sum to put aside for God. This means I can give as God directs and this has been a blessing. Otherwise, we have a joint account that he controls."

Only 5 percent of the wives who completed my questionnaire, however, referred to money as one of the problem areas between themselves and their husbands. This suggests that Christian wives absorb any pressure put on them at church, rather than taking it home and allowing it to affect their relationship with their husbands. When this happens, they may feel as if they are wedged between three pressures: a husband who may have firm views about how the family's money is spent; the needs of their church as expressed by the leaders; and the teaching God has given in the Bible.

The Old Testament teaches us about tithes and offerings, the old covenant structures for giving to God. The New Testament tells us that since Jesus came to earth, his disciples are equally obliged to give to God generously. Paul told the church in Corinth that "On the first day of every week, each one of you should set aside a sum of money in keeping with his income" (1 Cor 16:2).

The problem is not that these wives do not want to give or will not give; it is often that they cannot. Many do not hold the family purse strings apart from general housekeeping monies, and because they are married to a husband who is not a Christian, they do not have any right to give this money to God. To do so without his agreement may lead to two extra problems: the family may suffer deprivation and the wife may feel that she is being deceitful. These wives, therefore, cannot give to the church as other Christians do, and this makes them feel guilty.

Derek and Lilian Cook report on the reaction of one wife. "We're not short of money," she says, "but I find it difficult to give money to things I know my husband wouldn't agree with." The Cooks make some constructive suggestions about ways in which a wife may be able to handle this kind of delicate situation:

1. Look out for appeals from good causes that you think your husband *would* approve of. Often Christians are involved in such projects. Get your husband's agreement before you give.

2. Buy gifts and books from Christian sources where profits are ploughed back into Christian work.

3. Even if your husband brings home all the earnings in your home, recognize that if you received a salary for all the work you do, he could probably not afford to pay you. This means that you have actually earned some of it, and it is therefore fair for you to allocate some of it.

4. If you have the time, shop around at various supermarkets for goods you need, and buy at the cheapest price. You may feel that you have the right to allocate the money you save in any way you wish.[7]

The suggestions made so far assume that the wife with an uncommitted husband will have to find ways of dealing with insensitive church leaders who, unknowingly, will often impose hurt and guilt on her. It will be much better when leaders recognize problems in advance, speak more sensitively, and free wives from such feelings by clarifying when speaking about church finances.

Discourage new mixed marriages by teaching Scripture. When *Christian Family* conducted a survey of readers from homes where one partner was a believer and the other was not, they discovered that just under a quarter (24 percent) of the wives had been Christians when they married.[8] My own research shows that 33 percent of those completing questionnaires were Christians when they married non-Christian partners. These marriages took place despite the unequivocal teaching of Scripture.

When writing to Christians in Corinth, Paul draws attention to the radical difference between those who have a relationship with Christ and those who do not. "What do righteousness and wickedness have in common? Or what fellowship can light have with darkness?" he asks (2 Cor 6:14). In the same verse he highlights a real-life situation to which we must apply his teaching: "Do not be yoked together with unbelievers." In saying this, he rules out marriages between Christians and unbelievers. He argues that the two are spiritually incompatible because of what Christ has done in the life of the Christian.

This endorses teaching under the old covenant about marriage between Jews and those of other races. God made it clear that this was wholly unacceptable (Dt 7:3-4) because it would lead to compromise and a dilution of the believers' faith. Nowhere is this more obvious than in the marriage of the Jewish king, Ahab, to Jezebel, daughter of the king of Sidon. It seems that Ahab wasted little time before he "began to serve Baal and worship him. He set up an altar for Baal in the temple of Baal that he built in Samaria" (1 Kgs 16:31-32). This offended God greatly.

Along with many other Bible teachers and counselors, and with no intention of being critical or unkind, I believe that when Christians and unbelievers marry, it is in disobedience to God. There is enormous wisdom in the biblical teaching prohibiting spiritually mixed marriages for, as we saw earlier, much pain and hurt often accompanies such relationships. Not only this, but the Christian's spiritual life often does not develop fully if he or she becomes involved romantically with someone who does not share the faith.

Everyone's heard of the Christian girl who goes out with a non-Christian who then becomes a Christian. But the sad fact is that for every time it happens that way round, there are 100 occasions when the Christian ends up getting pulled away from God and even abandons their faith altogether. It's hard enough living for Christ anyway. The last thing any of us need is someone pulling us in the opposite direction.[9]

It is never easy for church leaders to decline to marry a believer to an unbeliever, especially when they are eager to see the uncommitted partner find Christ. If the leaders agree to such a union, however, it suggests that they have a blatant disregard for God's Word, and are willing to compromise.

On the basis of Scripture, my conviction is that churches owe it to God, to their members, and to those asking for marriage, not only to teach this truth, but also to apply it in practice. Such a policy may not be popular with some people, but God honors those who seek to uphold his truth.

Teach biblical truth about all aspects of family life. The Bible contains God's mind and truth about most issues that affect twentieth-century life. It teaches about family life, human sexuality and morality, marriage, childrearing, and many other subjects. Christian congregations need to hear this kind of teaching today more than ever, and it is the responsibility of churches, and especially their senior leaders, to see that

God's people are aware of the truth of his Word. Christians can only submit themselves to God's way if they are aware of his perspective on the issues that affect them.

In an era when many marriages fail, Christians need teaching about God's view of divorce. According to the Bible, a married Christian cannot consider divorce and remarriage as an option, unless the Christian's partner has been sexually unfaithful (Mt 19:9). God views adultery as the breaking of a covenant made when the marriage was established. Tim LaHaye observes that "the minute that pledge is broken, they have severed their commitment. In the Old Testament such individuals were to be taken out and stoned to death, which reflects the seriousness of the crime in the eyes of God."[10]

The fact that divorce, remarriage, and cohabitation are now commonplace in Western society is no reason for Christians to accept them. The prime responsibility of Christians is to be loyal to God's truth as revealed in Scripture. Congregations need teaching about what is out of bounds for believers, and what God delights to share with us because he loves us.

The Bible is a rich spiritual resource, and if any church is to serve its adherents responsibly, it must declare God's truth boldly. This is one of the main ways in which God's people will receive the teaching they need.

CONCLUSION

In these five ways, at least, churches can show Christian wives with husbands who do not share their faith that they are committed to helping them. They also show that, in an increasingly pagan world, they are dedicated to taking seriously the standards of marital and family life which Scripture teaches.

Above everything else, two things are crucially important. First, every Christian wife whose husband does not believe in Christ must continue to develop and grow as a Christian.

Wives will make most headway when they are part of a local church and receive support and encouragement there. Second, every uncommitted husband must have the opportunity to make a response to the gospel. He cannot do this if he has not heard the Good News of Jesus. Also, if his wife professes personal faith in Christ, but does not reflect this in her daily life, he is far less likely to make a Christian commitment himself.

I have no doubt that God's ideal is that there should be no spiritually mixed marriages. New ones should not be started, and, because God deeply loves all unsaved people, the existing ones should undergo a profound change when the uncommitted partner responds in faith to Christ. This is what we pray for and seek.

I asked Christian wives whose husbands have not yet responded to Christ what they thought would change if their husbands became Christians. Fiona thinks "everything" in their relationship would change. "I think it would bring us closer together and hopefully we would have a shared social life that is not very good at the moment. I would love to be able to pray together with my husband instead of struggling on my own."

Marilyn has recently celebrated her silver wedding anniversary. When she married her husband, she did not do so lightly. "It concerned me that he didn't share my faith, but I loved him." Eventually, she accepted his marriage proposal because she was fearful that no one else would ever ask her. She did so, however, "with one important condition—that he was not to stop me going to church. In return, I was not to stop him from pursuing his hobby (scuba diving)."

Now, over twenty-five years later, she says, "By and large they have been enjoyable years. However, I would imagine that being married to a fellow Christian would make for a far richer life together than ours has been. It grieves me that he is not aware of the love and peace that can be found in a wonderful relationship with our Lord. It grieves me, too, that I might well have been able to serve the Lord more fully than I have. I pray continually that the scales will fall from his eyes and that one day soon he will be able to share my faith."

Maybe God will answer Fiona's and Marilyn's prayers one day. Perhaps yours will be answered too. Jesus teaches us that God notices those who pray persistently (Lk 11:5-8; 18:1-8) and honors this. I hope and pray that the day will come when this book becomes irrelevant and unnecessary for you because your husband is moved by the Holy Spirit to trust in Jesus as you do!

While the research that I undertook for this book was essentially qualitative and not quantitative, I have gathered some statistical information which may be of interest to some readers.

From the 131 questionnaires that I received back from Christian wives with husbands who do not share their faith, the following facts emerged:

1. The age of the participants.

8% were in their 20s	15% were in their 50s
30% were in their 30s	9% were in their 60s
36% were in their 40s	2% were in their 70s

2. The length of time participating wives have been married.

24% less than 11 years	9% from 31-40 years
35% from 11-20 years	6% from 41-50 years
26% from 21-30 years	0% more than 50 years

3. Whether the participants were Christians when they married.

33% were Christians
59% were not Christians
8% said they were backslidden Christians

4. The proportion of participating wives who are mothers.
87%

5. Whether the Christian participants have had to make one or more visits to a doctor or counselor because of problems with the non-Christian husband.
18% have had to seek professional help
82% have not had to seek professional help

6. Whether the Christian participants have used prescription medication because of problems with the non-Christian husband.
6% have used prescription medication
94% have not used prescription medication

7. Whether the husbands of participants attend any church events.
9% often attend church events
55% occasionally attend church events
36% never attend church events

8. Whether the participants' churches provide a special group for Christian wives whose husbands do not share their faith.
2% provide a special group
98% do not provide a special group

9. The proportion of participating wives who have the impression that more women than men become Christians.
82% believe that more women than men become Christians
7% do not believe that more women than men become Christians
11% do not know

NOTES

ONE
What Are You Going Through?

1. Lawrence J Crabb, *The Marriage Builder* (Navpress: New Malden, 1987), 18.
2. Crabb, 17.
3. Sandra Carter, "Conflict of Faith," *Christian Family* (March 1991), 14.
4. Derek and Lilian Cook, video *Husbands and the Kingdom* (Maranatha Ministries: Kirkby Stephen, 1992), tape 1.
5. Carter, 14.
6. Lilian Cook, "What does your partner think about your Faith? Part 2: Husbands and their Reactions," *Christian Family* (May 1992), 14.
7. Carter, 14.
8. Carter, 14.
9. Lilian Cook, 14.
10. Linda Davis, *How to Be the Happy Wife of an Unsaved Husband* (Whitaker: Springdale), 142.

TWO
How Does This Affect You?

1. Michael J. Fanstone, *The Sheep That Got Away* (Monarch: Tunbridge Wells, 1993), 62.
2. Davis, 65-66.
3. D.W. Winnicott, *The Child, the Family, and the Outside World* (Penguin Books: Harmondsworth, 1964), 180.

THREE
How Can God Help You?

1. Lilian Cook, 12.
2. Carter, 15.
3. James Engel, "What's Gone Wrong With the Harvest?" (Zondervan) reproduced in an adapted form in *Evangelism Explosion/Teach and Reach Handbook* (Southampton, 1981), 104.

4. Davis, 95-96.
5. Crabb, 109.
6. Davis, 104.

FOUR
What Is Your Husband Going Through?

1. Jim Smith, "Save the Male," *Buzz* (April 1987), 30.
2. Bridget Hall, "My husband doesn't understand...," *Woman Alive* (February 1992), 15.
3. Gavin Wakefield, "Barriers that keep men out of our churches," *Christian Woman* (December 1988), 25-29.
4. Wakefield, 25-29.
5. Davis, 50-51.
6. Davis, 51.
7. Davis, 51.
8. Wakefield, 25.
9. Davis, 39-40.
10. Davis, 39.
11. Derek and Lilian Cook, *Husbands and the Kingdom*, tape 1.
12. Joyce Huggett, "Lost in Faith," *Christian Family* (June 1989), 36.
13. Huggett, 36.
14. David Bennett, "An Open Letter from a Church Widower," *Christian Woman* (December 1988), 47.
15. Carter, 14.
16. Carter, 14.
17. Derek and Lilian Cook, "Just you, me and my Friend called Jesus," *Woman Alive* (May 1991), 25.
18. Lilian Cook, 12.
19. Derek and Lilian Cook, "Just you, me and my Friend called Jesus," 26.
20. Lilian Cook, 12.

FIVE
How Can You Help Your Husband?

1. Christine Noble, "Walls of Lies," *Christian Family* (March 1990), 12.
2. Derek and Lilian Cook, *Husbands and the Kingdom*, tape 1.
3. *The Alternative Service Book 1980* (Clowes, SPCK, Cambridge University Press: Colchester, 1980), 290.

4. Joyce Huggett, "Lop-Sided Love," *Christian Family* (June 1987), 14.

5. Naomi Starkey, "Whatever Happened to Fun?" *Christian Family* (November 1992), 28.

6. Huggett, 15.

7. Starkey, 28.

8. Derek and Lilian Cook, *Husbands and the Kingdom,* tape 2.

9. Derek and Lilian Cook, *Husbands and the Kingdom,* tape 2.

10. Wakefield, 26.

11. Wakefield, 26-27.

12. Wakefield, 27.

13. Derek and Lilian Cook, *Husbands and the Kingdom,* tape 2.

SIX
What Effects Do Children Feel?

1. D.W. Winnicott, 227.

2. Rosemary Wells, *Helping Children Cope with Divorce* (Sheldon Press: London, 1989), 4-5.

3. Steve Hepden, *Explaining Rejection* (Sovereign World: Tonbridge, 1992), 46-47.

4. Winnicott, 228.

SEVEN
How Can You Help Your Children?

1. Wells, 10.

2. Wells, 13.

3. Wells, 26.

EIGHT
How Can Your Church Help You?

1. Fanstone, 62.

2. Derek and Lilian Cook, "Just you, me and my friend called Jesus," 29.

3. Davis, 137.

4. Davis, 143.

5. Lilian Cook, 9.

6. Carter, 15.

7. Derek and Lilian Cook, *Husbands and the Kingdom,* tape 1.
8. Lilian Cook, 8.
9. Steve Chalke, "The 21CC Guide Book for Valentines," *21st Century Christian* (February 1989), 17.
10. Tim LaHaye, *I Love You, but Why Are We So Different?* (Kingsway: Eastbourne, 1992), 191.

The following is a list of titles which cover many of the subjects raised in this book.

Auch, Ron. *Prayer Can Change Your Marriage.* Green Forest, Ark.: New Leaf Press, 1990.

Christenson, Evelyn. *What Happens when We Pray for Our Families.* Wheaton, Ill.: Scripture Press, 1992.

Crabb, Lawrence J. *The Marriage Builder: A Blueprint for Couples and Counselors.* Grand Rapids, Mich.: Zondervan, 1992.

Davis, Linda. *How to be the Happy Wife of an Unsaved Husband.* Springdale, Penn.: Whitaker House, 1986.

Heald, Cynthia. *Loving Your Husband: Building an Intimate Marriage in A Fallen World.* Colorado Springs: NavPress, 1989.

Heald, Jack and Cynthia. *Loving Your Wife: Building an Intimate Marriage in a Fallen World.* Colorado Springs: NavPress, 1989.

LaHaye, Tim. *I Love You, but Why Are We So Different?* Eugene, Ore.: Harvest House, 1991.

Mason, Mike. *The Mystery of Marriage: As Iron Sharpens Iron.* Sisters, Ore.: Questar, 1985.

Smalley, Gary and John Trent. *The Two Sides of Love.* Colorado Springs: Focus on the Family, 1992.

Strauss, Richard and Mary. *When Two Walk Together: Learning to Communicate Love and Acceptance in Your Marriage.* Nashville, Tenn.: Nelson, 1988.

Winnicott, Donald W. *The Child, the Family, and the Outside World*. Reading, Mass.: Addison-Wesley, 1992.